# THEIR
# *Darkest Hour*

*To Rupert Harding*

# THEIR
# *Darkest Hour*

## THE HIDDEN HISTORY
## OF THE HOME FRONT
## 1939–1945

## STUART HYLTON

SUTTON PUBLISHING

First published in the United Kingdom in 2001 by
Sutton Publishing Limited · Phoenix Mill
Thrupp · Stroud · Gloucestershire · GL5 2BU

British Library Cataloguing in Publication Data
A catalogue record for this book is available from the British Library.

ISBN 0-7509-2522-1

Typeset in 10.5/13pt Photina MT.
Typesetting and origination by
Sutton Publishing Limited.
Printed and bound in England by
J.H. Haynes & Co. Ltd, Sparkford.

# CONTENTS

For nine months the land war had been a stalemate – while the home front had been a dreary catalogue of restrictions, regulations, frustrations and aggravations, all of which had achieved absolutely nothing. The German Blitzkrieg arrived just at the time when the 'Bore War', as it was dubbed, had reduced most of the civilian population to apathy. Home Intelligence reports . . . again and again reported apathy, boredom and irritation with the civil defence preparations. . . .

In March 1940, one person in ten was in favour of stopping the war immediately. . . .

Peter Lewis, discussing the state of the nation at the time of Dunkirk (*A People's War*, Thames Methuen, 1986)

# INTRODUCTION

Rationing, blackouts, bombs, shortages of everything . . . such a diet would soon have destroyed the spirit of the people in most countries, but to the surprise and niggling annoyance of the Nazi regime, little Britain kept its pecker up and kept hitting back. Instead of whining and bemoaning its lot, we whistled as we worked and kept our spirits up with a string of memorable songs, both humorous and sentimental. If anything, the only secret weapon we ever possessed was our crackpot sense of humour which saw the funny side of almost everything. It flourished everywhere . . . at the Front, at work, in the bus queue and even in the air raid shelter. It became stronger under the most trying circumstances, and it was this as much as anything else which enabled us to 'keep on keeping on', and so led to the ultimate defeat of Hitler.

Roy Faiers, 'This was their finest hour',
This England, *Summer 1994*

Growing up as I did just after the Second World War, my picture of the home front during the war years was gained largely from the films of the time. Like the writer quoted above, I carried in my head a composite image of chirpy cockneys in the Anderson shelter, singing along to Vera Lynn on the radio as they made do and mended and the bombs burst all around them.

That image was dispelled for me in no uncertain terms several years ago, when I wrote a book about the war years as they were experienced in Reading, the town where I now live. My idealised picture was replaced by a reassuringly mixed view of the people and the times, in which grumbles, incompetence, bureaucracy and opportunism lived alongside the sacrifice and bravery that was undoubtedly part of the experience of those years.

This book stems from that revelation, and is my personal antidote to the excessive sentimentality which still exists in some quarters about the war years. It does not in any way aim to belittle the contribution those at home made to the war effort. But what it does try to do is to remind us that Britain won the war despite the best efforts of the bureaucrats, defeatists, profiteers and bigots among them.

In writing this, I was extremely fortunate in the wealth of published material available on the period, and I have included a section on my sources for the different parts of the book later on. In addition, I found a lot of material in local and national newspapers of the time. Two other contemporary sources were important to me, as they were for many other historians of the war before me.

Home Intelligence was, from early 1940, the Ministry of Information's machinery for keeping the government apprised of the thinking of the home population through the war years. They drew upon information gleaned by censors, looking at letters and monitoring telephone conversations; reports compiled by thirteen regional officers; bar room chatter and newspaper reports; grievances raised via MPs; reports from police duty rooms; BBC listener research; and talk picked up in newsagents and cinemas, and by agencies such as the WVS and the Citizens' Advice Bureau. Another important source for Home Intelligence was Mass Observation, set up in 1936 by Frank Jennings, Tom Harrisson and Charles Madge to apply anthropological techniques to the study of the home population. They started out by advertising in the New Statesman for volunteers to observe the views and behaviour of the public.

Thanks are due to the *Evening Standard* for permission to quote from the captions to the wartime cartoons of that splendidly satirical old bigot, Colonel Blimp. With one exception, the photographs in this book are reproduced with the permission of the Trustees of the Imperial War Museum, London. The one exception, the picture of bomb damage in Reading, is reproduced with the permission of Reading Central Library, which is part of Reading Borough Council. I have made every effort to track down any third party copyright, but if any have been inadvertently missed, please let me know via the publisher.

Last but by no means least, thanks are due to Rupert Harding, my editor at Suttons for this book and most of my previous work for them. In recognition of his help and encouragement over many years, this book is dedicated to him.

# ONE

# OVER HERE: INTERNEES, ALIENS, FIFTH COLUMNISTS

The Nazis keep their concentration camps for their enemies; we use them for our friends.

*G.M. Trevelyan in a letter to* The Times

## ALIENS IN THE FIRST WORLD WAR

The treatment of foreign nationals living in Britain was one of the least glorious episodes of the First World War. About 67,000 Germans and Austrians were registered with the police by 9 September 1914, and at that time the government found good reason to intern only a tiny number of them. But by the spring of 1915 stories of atrocities in Europe, the Zeppelin raids and a hate campaign run by the newspapers led to mob violence towards 'foreigners'. Businesses owned by, or employing, Germans were attacked, foreigners were assaulted and the escalation of violence in the streets of Liverpool and West Ham after the sinking of the *Lusitania* resulted in 257 casualties.

Nobody was too great or too insignificant to evade the mob's anger. At one extreme, Prince Louis Battenberg, First Sea Lord and a distinguished public servant, was hounded out of office as a result of his German antecedents. At the other, innocent dachshunds found themselves being kicked in the street for the same reason. In May 1915 a petition bearing 250,000 signatures was presented to Parliament, calling for the immediate arrest of all aliens of military age. The government responded with large-scale internment – by the end of that year, some 32,274 were behind bars, and the last of them was not released until long after the war was over, in September 1919.

The scars that this left made many people determined to avoid similar excesses in the conflict that was brewing twenty years later. Viscount Cobham, the Under-Secretary of State for War, told the House of Lords on 24 October 1939 that:

It is not likely to happen, as there are far fewer enemy aliens, especially of military age, in this country than there were at the commencement of the last war, in spite of all the refugees. The figure I have been given, as being likely to be interned as enemy aliens, is somewhere between 1,000 and 1,500, as against a figure of over 29,000 during the last war.

## ALIENS IN THE SECOND WORLD WAR

Britain's response to the German refugee problem in the run-up to the war was an honourable one. They accepted them in large numbers, at a time when many other countries refused them admission. By the outbreak of war, there were over sixty thousand refugees in Britain, in addition to other foreign nationals. Most were of German or Austrian origin and about half of them had come in during the nineteen months preceding the outbreak of war.

Tribunals were set up across the country in the early days of the war to identify those who were regarded as a potential threat to national security. They were classified into three groups. In Category A were those who were openly hostile to Britain, and they were to be interned within days of war starting. In Category B were the borderline cases, in particular those who had only recently arrived in the country. The remainder, Category C, had been in the country for at least six years and were generally political or racial refugees from Hitler.

The Tribunals started work in October 1939 and it soon became clear that there was considerable inconsistency in their decisions. One put all domestic servants into Category B, while another immediately interned anyone who was a socialist or a communist. Some interned anyone they thought would be vulnerable to blackmail, lest they be forced to act as German spies; others were locked up because they were in sensitive occupations. Some cases turned purely on chance factors: one man was thought to have been 'shopped' as a Fifth Columnist by a rival who wanted his job as a piano player. In another case a German who spoke no English was examined by a Tribunal which spoke no German, without the benefit of an interpreter. He was immediately interned on suspicion of being foreign.

The government had to issue additional guidance to try to standardise the results. Of the final total of 73,355 cases examined, 66,002 were put into Category C. Some 55,000 of these were recorded as refugees from Nazi persecution. The great majority of the remainder were category B and only 569 were classed as definite security risks.

Category B aliens were subject to a variety of controls. Their movements were restricted, they were subject to a curfew and could not own such things as maps, a wireless, a car or a bike. Thus, one Johannes Hofels found himself fined the considerable sum (for the day) of £10 plus 5 guineas (£5.25) costs for possessing maps of parts of Britain. Hofels, who was 65 and had lived in Britain since 1901, had been a member of the Auf Wiedersehen Rambling Club before the war. The club had been set up to

FRIENDLY ALIEN

German Jewish Cambridge undergraduate Mark Lynton (formerly Max-Otto Loewenstein) recalls with amusement his Tribunal, in front of half a dozen First World War vintage officers and a judge. He was armed with a letter from General Sir Ernest Swinton, saying that he would be a reference for Lynton, despite never having met him: 'This geriatric gaggle set to in the finest Colonel Blimp tradition: What school had I been to (Cheltenham; very sound); did I play soccer or rugby there (rugby, of course; very good); did I play squash (I did; splendid); was I a member of the Officer Training Corps (forgot it was Cheltenham; silly question, of course, ha-ha); what was I studying in Cambridge (law; bit odd that, brainy chap, what? never mind). It went on in that vein until it came to references, and I handed over Swinton's note. Just as Guillebaud had forecast, it was reverently passed from hand to hand ("Sir Ernest? Why, I met him once near Cambrai in 1917"), and I was promptly certified as a "friendly alien".'

promote Anglo-German friendship, but had understandably ceased activity in 1939.

Another case which attracted considerable interest was that of Wilhelm Solf, an Oxford student. The son of the former German Ambassador to Japan under the Weimar Republic, he was given a month's imprisonment, followed by internment, for photographing a crashed German plane. The case led to no fewer than four editorials, calling for a review of Category B aliens, in the *Daily Mail*.

## THE MYTH OF THE FIFTH COLUMN

It is extraordinary how we get circumstantial reports of Fifth Columnists and yet we have never been able to get anything worth having. One is persuaded that it hardly exists. And yet there is signalling going on all over the place and we cannot get any evidence.

General Ironside, C-in-C Home Forces.

General Ironside illustrates the willingness of the authorities to believe in the existence of the Fifth Column in the absence of *any* evidence to support it. Lord Haw-Haw's* apparently intimate knowledge of events in Britain

---

* Lord Haw-Haw was the name given to a number of broadcasters on the German propaganda stations, but it is primarily associated with William Joyce – *see* p. 74.

was often held to be proof of its existence, yet a Ministry of Information investigation in January 1941 could find 'no case . . . in which Haw Haw or any German wireless made predictions regarding a specific place or announced any detailed facts which . . . could not have been obtained through an explicable channel'.

The term Fifth Column came from the Spanish Civil War, when Nationalist General Emilio Moro claimed to have four armies converging on Madrid and a fifth column of secret nationalist sympathisers ready to support their cause within Madrid itself. Even in its first incarnation, the claim was untrue. It was designed to spread alarm and confusion among the opposing armies, and it had its desired effect, leading to a witch hunt and a self-inflicted purge among the opposition. The idea was a potent – but more or less totally groundless – one throughout the war years in Britain. No rumour was too wild to be denied circulation, though the story of a house full of blind alien refugees all being secretly armed with machine-guns must have stretched some people's credulity.

As Hitler made his way across Europe, the media eagerly reported the activities of Nazi sympathisers, real or imagined, in the countries that were overrun. This extract from the *Daily Express* account of the invasion of the Low Countries:

> As machine-guns came out of the sky like unnatural lightning, peppering the streets below, the Fifth Column crept out of their homes in their German uniforms, heavily armed. Holland had combed out the Fifth Column for weeks before but as the doors opened at 3 a.m. the men who had been proclaimed anti-Nazis and refugees from Germany held rifles.

In fact, German attempts to plant spies in Britain, both before and during the war, were quite spectacularly unsuccessful. Those few spies in place before the outbreak of hostilities were rounded up within the first few hours of war. A further two dozen or more were landed by boat or plane in September 1940. Almost without exception, they were captured within hours. Many were taken to a camp called 020 (the roman numerals for which are XX – or 'double cross'), which was run by MI5. The threat of the death penalty often persuaded the captured agents to 'turn' and work for the allies. One, a Dane called Wolf Schmidt, became the British agent 'Tate', and was able to persuade the Germans of the existence of a bogus minefield in the North Atlantic, to the great benefit of the convoys.

But the most successful of the turned spies was a Spaniard, Juan Pujol, codenamed 'Garbo'. He had applied to be a British spy but was turned down, so he pursued his career in espionage with the Abwehr, the German military intelligence organisation. His operating base for the Germans was the espionage capital of Europe – Lisbon – though the Abwehr thought he

---

STATELESS

In September 1939 all Germans living abroad received call-up papers for the armed forces. They were issued regardless of religion, race and other considerations. When, understandably, the refugee population in Britain did not respond to the call-up, the German authorities revoked their citizenship. The British government's response to this was to say that the German government's decree 'did not count' and that, in the British view, they were still Germans. This left the refugees technically stateless. When, later in the war, some of the refugees went on to serve in the allied armed forces, they were actually serving as what the British Government defined as 'enemy aliens'.

---

was actually in London. The British took him on and brought him back to England, where he ran a network of imaginary sub-agents (including one called Lady Smith-Jones) in a manner later associated more with soap opera producers.

Garbo's greatest triumph related to D-Day, when he managed to invent a whole army – the First United States Army Group, or FUSAG – and persuade the Germans that the main landing point was to be in the Pas de Calais. Not only this, but once the Operation Overlord landings in Normandy were under way, he even convinced them that Overlord was merely a diversion for the bigger landing that was to come. Thus, he delayed the Germans sending reinforcements to Normandy. Later, he was able to send back misleading information about the landing points of the V1 flying bombs, causing the Germans to make future flights fall short. For all these services to the German war effort, Garbo was awarded the Iron Cross in the final months of the war.

From the earliest days of the war there was lobbying for internment on a large scale. Lord Hailsham (the father of the politician Quintin Hogg) warned the House of Lords in November 1939 against interning only those against whom charges could be proved. Those left at liberty would, he said, guide the enemy, start fires and disrupt the work of the ARP authorities. But in general terms the *Spectator* on 19 January 1940 was still able to praise the absence of a witch hunt to any significant degree.

Early in 1940 scare stories began to appear in the press about the activities of the Fifth Column. The *Daily Sketch* blamed them for mysterious explosions in a gunpowder factory at Waltham Cross (20 January 1940), while the *Sunday Express* claimed that Germans in Britain were being blackmailed – by threats to their families at home – into spying (21 January 1940).

It was as the Germans broke through in the west that a hysterical campaign was begun in both the press and the corridors of government to imprison *all* enemy aliens. There were ulterior motives for both sources of pressure. The leading papers in whipping up anti-Fifth Column feeling were for the most part those owned by pre-war pro-Nazis and appeasers. During the 1930s Lord Rothermere, who owned the *Sunday Dispatch* and the *Daily Mail*, had been a staunch supporter of Hitler as a 'bulwark against bolshevism', had run pro-fascist campaigns and was the patron of Princess Stephanie von Hohenloe, a confidante of Hitler who was eventually arrested in America by the FBI and interned. With the outbreak of war, such attitudes became deeply unfashionable, not to say embarrassing, and it may have been in an attempt to cover his tracks that Rothermere took such an aggressively anti-alien standpoint. Another press baron notable for his attacks on the aliens was another former appeaser, Viscount Kemsley, owner of the *Sunday Times* and other papers.

The rapid invasion of Norway and Denmark took British Intelligence by complete surprise, despite a wealth of evidence about Hitler's intentions, which they chose to ignore or misinterpret. Rather than admit their mistakes, intelligence sources preferred to blame a well-developed Fifth Column for the speed of Norway's collapse. Their case was given valuable impetus by the brief emergence of Vidkun Quisling, the former Norwegian War Minister turned Nazi collaborator, whose real influence was actually so minimal that he was kept in the dark about German plans before the invasion (General von Falkenhurst, in charge of the German invasion forces, had never even heard of him) and was largely ignored afterwards. American reports of a massive Trojan horse of Fifth Columnists, created by the Germans before the invasion, were based on the flimsiest of what turned out to be incorrect evidence, but such reports gained widespread and unquestioning acceptance in Britain. This extract from the *Yorkshire Post* in April 1940 gives an example of how the spectre of the Fifth Column was raised with a minimum of hard evidence and a maximum of innuendo:

> Before attacking a country, Hitler always tries to undermine it from within. How does he enlist his sympathisers, ready to work for him when the hour strikes? Partly by a long continued policy of threats, which compels the chosen country to allow the organisation of a Nazi party, raised around a nucleus of German nationals in its midst. Partly by spreading fears of invasion, which tempt the unscrupulous and timorous to ensure their good standing with the invaders in advance. Local adventurers and ne'er-do-wells are attracted by the promise of fat jobs when the Nazis arrive.

The *Sunday Dispatch*, as the following extract shows, made particular attacks on communist sympathisers and members of pacifist organisations such as the Peace Pledge Union, whom they dubbed 'conchies' . . . who constitute 'an underground political force which endangers the very life of the nation':

> The seriousness of the menace in Glasgow, second city of the British Empire, can be judged from the message to the *Sunday Dispatch* from Lord Provost Dollan:
> Here there are more than two thousand subversive agents acting on instructions from Moscow. They disguise themselves as peace societies or genuine working class organisations. It is time they were shown up for what they are.

Nothing was too insubstantial or peripheral for them to use. The *Dispatch* ran stories about the pampered treatment alien internees received in prison and retailed backstairs gossip from domestic servants, whose (unnamed) German colleagues seemed to spend a good deal of time near important military establishments. Another day, the target would be Czech refugees who were spending government money on the production of (no doubt subversive) leaflets.

One of the most loathsome specimens in the field of anti-alien polemic was the writer Beverley Nichols, described by François Lafitte (author of the best-selling book of the time on internment) as 'ex-pacifist, ex-Buckmanite, ex-Mosley supporter, ex-pro Nazi'. This is one example of Nichols's work, from the *Sunday Chronicle* of 11 May 1941:

> Cast your eye for a moment on the Isle of Man; a delectable spot with plenty of good food; a spot where many of us would like to spend a short holiday. Well, there are some people who are spending a very long holiday there at the British taxpayers' expense, but they are not British. They are interned aliens, all avowed or suspected enemies of this country. The manner in which they are being coddled is driving many people on the island pretty well crazy. Our treatment of these people carries humanitarianism to the verge of insanity. . . .

Nichols goes on to speculate about the internees being allowed to breed generations of new Nazis in their mixed camps, a thought which must have been offensive and bewildering in equal proportions to the many middle-aged Jews living in their overcrowded, sexually segregated camps on the island. The *Daily Mail* also appealed on behalf of a 'public opinion' of their own invention: 'Disquiet about Britain's "Fifth Column" is growing . . . the people ask that doubtful enemy aliens should be immediately interned and all other aliens strictly examined. . . . The traitors of Norway have shown the perils of the enemy within.'

For good measure, the same article also alleged that the public were crying out for action against communists and 'peace cranks'. Extremes of public opinion were indiscriminately given space in the papers. One local paper carried a call for concentration camps to be established for enemy aliens in Britain, while the *Daily Mail* published a letter calling for them to wear distinctive armbands – a chilling echo of the Star of David that Hitler forced Jews to wear in public places in Germany.

Not all the newspapers were so rabid in their positions. *The Times* opposed large-scale internment in an editorial on 23 April 1940, and the *Daily Express* spoke out in ringing terms in favour of 'freedom' and 'liberty'. The latter's position may have been not entirely unconnected with the fact that its proprietor, Lord Beaverbrook, was having a relationship with a Jewish refugee at the time.

Mass Observation carried out a rather more systematic sampling of public opinion about the Fifth Column at about the same time. Far from the public baying for blood:

> We found that the majority of the people hardly recognised what the phrase meant. We also found that the level of ordinary people's feelings was much less intense than that expressed in some papers. Detailed interviewing in several areas in London and Western Scotland produced less than one person in a hundred who spontaneously suggested that refugees ought to be interned en masse.

Politicians none the less began to join the hue and cry. On 19 April some seventy Conservative MPs met at the Commons to discuss the problem of the Fifth Column. Some Labour MPs also became concerned, though their perspective on the problem was rather different. Whereas the Conservatives aimed their fire at aliens, communists and pacifists, the focus of Labour's concern was Oswald Mosley and the groups on the political far right. *Reynolds News*, which numbered Richard Crossman and J.B. Priestley among its editorial staff, was one of the few papers to follow the more socialist line. Crossman wrote that the Fifth Column would be found among: 'the rich and respected of the land. I can only explain the arrest of Social Democrats from Nazi concentration camps as a hysterical attempt to persuade public opinion that something is being done about a Fifth Column. It arouses my suspicion.'

However, *Reynolds News* and some of the papers on the left ran a campaign against British Fifth Columnists which was sometimes scarcely more responsible than that of the right-wing papers against the aliens. The *Manchester Guardian* became a particular champion of the refugees. By the end of 1940 they had published some 54 articles and leaders and 110 (overwhelmingly supportive) letters on the subject.

Some in the Civil Service shared the suspicion that the hysteria against enemy aliens was a blind to disguise real Fifth Column activity by British-born Nazi sympathisers. Moves were made to try to have aliens simply resettled as free people in other countries, rather than deported and interned. This was rejected, on the grounds that public opinion would not stand for such preferential treatment. If the German invasion were successful, the powers-that-be decided, the aliens should 'go down in the common ruin'.

At the same time as they tried to calm public sentiment, staff at the Home Office were being pressured by the security services. The latter maintained their belief in the danger of the Fifth Column, despite the lack of evidence. As a Joint Intelligence Committee report saw it, the absence of sabotage to date was some kind of bizarre proof of the existence of Fifth Columnists:

> We cannot rule out the possibility that Fifth Column activities in this country, at present dormant, might well play a very active and highly dangerous part at the appropriate moment selected by the enemy . . . the absence of sabotage up to date reinforces the view that such activities will only take place as part of a prearranged military plan.

Winston Churchill became Prime Minister on the same day that the Low Countries were invaded. This invasion again provided boundless (and mostly false) evidence of Fifth Column activity, much of it from people who should have known better. These included members of the Dutch government and their royal family (whose official report to their counterparts at Buckingham Palace made it clear that it was Dutch natives of a Nazi disposition, and not German nationals living within their borders, who had been the real problem – insofar as a Fifth Column could be held accountable at all for the invasion).

Particularly culpable was Sir Nevile Bland, the British Minister to Holland. He fled as the Germans invaded, and presented the Foreign Secretary, Lord Halifax, with a scaremongering story of murderous paratroops and Fifth Column activity – a story that enjoyed a wide currency in Britain. It was circulated immediately to the Cabinet, prompting Winston Churchill to call in Cabinet for:

> A very large round up of enemy aliens and suspect persons . . . it would be much better that these persons should be behind barbed wire. . . . Internment would probably be much safer for all German-speaking persons themselves since, when air attacks develop, public temper in this country would be such that such persons would be in great danger if at liberty.

Churchill's bullish approach to the internment of aliens was particularly ironic, given that the refugee population had generally been among his strongest supporters, bitterly opposed to the appeasement policies of Chamberlain.

Bland compounded his errors by repeating them on the radio and, via the Ministry of Information, to the press. Despite admitting to the Chaplain to the British Legation in The Hague that he could not identify a single case where a German refugee acted as a Fifth Columnist in Holland, Bland advised his listeners: 'Be careful at this moment how you put complete trust in any person of German or Austrian connection . . . if you know people of this kind, who are at large, keep an eye on them.' In fact, the example of Holland was fairly irrelevant to Britain in a variety of ways. They shared a land border with Germany and a hundred thousand totally unvetted Germans living in the country before war broke out. It would have been far easier to establish a Fifth Column there than in England.

All this hysteria delighted the Germans, who, learning of this new and unexpected source of 'support' within Britain, wasted no time in getting Lord Haw-Haw to broadcast bogus instructions to his non-existent army of Fifth Columnists. This in turn increased the paranoia among the British population, and so the spiral of hysteria went on. The Ministry of Information managed to add to the problem. After reporting to the government on 5 June that 'Fifth Column hysteria is reaching quite dangerous proportions', they promptly made it worse by publishing their own leaflet on the subject, guaranteed to set neighbour against neighbour. It said:

> There is a Fifth Column in Britain. Anyone who thinks there isn't, that 'it can't happen here', has simply fallen into the trap laid by the Fifth Column itself. For the first job of the Fifth Column is to make people believe that it does not exist. In other countries, the most respectable and neighbourly citizens turned out to be Fifth Columnists.

The Home Secretary, Sir John Anderson, tried vainly to resist this tide of opinion. As a former career civil servant, he was opposed to large-scale internment as much on the grounds of the administrative chaos it would cause as for its injustice. The research his officials carried out found little or no evidence to support the allegations of others about Fifth Column activity, at home or abroad.

But, right at the height of the struggle within the Cabinet, news broke of a spying scandal involving Anna Wolkoff, a naturalised British woman of Russian extraction, and Tyler Kent, an American Embassy official. They were tried in secret at the Old Bailey and received long sentences. There was later a suggestion that at the heart of the case there was some kind of political conspiracy involving MI5. If so, it had the desired effect of hardening the climate of opinion against enemy aliens. By May 1940 Mass Observation was reporting a change in the public's views about aliens, often coupled with increasing anti-Semitism.

The Home Secretary finally lost his struggle against large-scale internment. On 27 May all Category B aliens of German or Austrian origin were ordered to be rounded up and arrested, followed by Category C males in the weeks following 21 June. Although much of the pressure for this came from the security forces, the blanket approach illustrated the failure of the government intelligence services to sort out the security risks from the genuine refugees. Nor was there any evidence to link refugees to specific pieces of Fifth Column activity. Last, but not least, it exposed the lie (for example, in the *Sunday Express* of 9 June 1940) that the authorities had seized a full list of all the potential Gauleiters-in-waiting and Fifth Columnists in a raid on the British Union of Fascists' office.

To complete the process, pressure was successfully exerted for alien women to be included in the round-up. *The Times*' leader of 23 May quoted Kipling's remark about the female of the species being deadlier than the male, while Beverley Nichols made his own, more basic, appeal to the public's fears: 'German women, some of them pretty, are not above offering their charms to any young man, particularly if he works in a munitions factory or in a public works.' By late May Churchill's position on internees had hardened yet further. By now, he was 'strongly in favour of removing all internees out of the United Kingdom.'

But worse was still to come.


## THE ITALIAN CONNECTION

Even before the Italians joined the war, they were being indiscriminately vilified. This example is from the *Daily Mirror* in April 1940:

> There are more than twenty thousand Italians in Great Britain. London alone shelters more than eleven thousand of them. The London Italian is an indigestible unit of population. He settles here more or less temporarily, working until he has enough money to buy himself a little land in Calabria, or Campagnia or Tuscany. He often avoids employing British labour. It is much cheaper to bring a few relations into England from the old home town.
>
> And so the boats unloaded all sorts of brown-eyed Francescas and Marias, beetle-browed Ginos, Titos and Marios. . . . Now every Italian colony in Great Britain and America is a seething cauldron of smoking Italian politics. Black fascism. Hot as hell.
>
> Even the peaceful, law-abiding proprietor of the back-street coffee shop bounces into a fine patriotic frenzy at the sound of Mussolini's name. . . . We are nicely honeycombed with little cells of potential betrayal. A storm is brewing in the Mediterranean. And we, in our droning silly tolerance, are helping it to gather force.

The treatment of the Italians was in some respects even more shameful than that of the other aliens. No real attempt was made even at the outset to screen them, to separate out the security risks from the others. The Acting Head of MI5, Brigadier Harker, wrote in May 1940:

> We have reason to suppose that the first act of war on the part of Italy might be an attempt to use the Italian fascist organisation for an attack on the key industries and key points in this country by the employment of gangster methods. We are therefore anxious that our arrangements should be made so as to forestall such attempts if possible.

They wanted the immediate arrest of 'all known suspects' and said that they had a list of 1,500 'desperate' and 'dangerous' characters. This list turned out to be fundamentally flawed. Not only did it include many prominent anti-fascists, it also failed to understand that membership of the Italian Fascists did not, in itself, make one 'desperate' and 'dangerous'. Even the Foreign Office understood this, as their memorandum from June 1940 shows:

> MI5's criteria for judging whether or not a person was a 'desperate character' more often than not resolved itself into mere membership of the Fascio. On being pointed out that membership of the Fascio was to all intents and purposes obligatory on any Italian resident abroad who desired to have any sort of claim to diplomatic or consular protection, they relented somewhat and limited their objection to Fascists of military age and special ardour. . . . As the discussion with MI5 proceeded there grew up a strong suspicion that in actual fact they had little or no information, let alone evidence, in regard to more than a fraction of the persons they had led the Home Secretary to describe to the Cabinet as 'desperate characters'.

But lack of evidence was not allowed to stand in the way. Immediately upon Mussolini's declaration of war, on 10 June 1940, Churchill issued the order 'Collar the lot!' Everyone on the MI5 list, plus all post-1919 residents, became eligible for internment. It was accompanied by a nationwide bout of xenophobic violence, reminiscent of the worst excesses of the First World War. The length and breadth of the country saw anti-Italian riots. Parts of Edinburgh were described as looking as if they had been bombed, and the police had to mount baton charges to disperse the crowds. Italian shops were wrecked and looted, in some cases with the terrified proprietors barricaded in upstairs. Children of Italian origin were victimised at school.

Italian businesses were quick to proclaim their loyalty. They would display signs saying 'this shop is entirely British' or 'the family owning this restaurant has sons serving in the British army'. Bianchis in Frith Street, Soho, changed overnight from an Italian to a Swiss restaurant and a Leeds organ grinder put up a sign saying 'I'm British and the monkey is from India'.

This xenophobia rebounded on the British in one respect. One of their favourite daughters, Gracie Fields, was forced to quit Britain for the United States before her Italian-born husband, Monty Banks, and she officially became 'enemy aliens'.

## THE INTERNMENT PROCESS

The process by which opinion was turned against alien refugees was disreputable enough, but the procedures by which they were detained were even more harsh and unjust. Even as Britain's ultimatum to Germany was running out, in September 1939, the exhibition halls at Olympia were being prepared for the reception of alien detainees. Arrests began even before war was formally declared, and the first batches rounded up on the instructions of MI5 contained an apparently random and potentially explosive mixture of ardent Nazis, Jews and political refugees. The latter included some people clearly arrested in error, such as Eugen Spier. As a member of the Focus for the Defence of Freedom and Peace before the war, Spier had advised Winston Churchill and helped inform his anti-appeasement stance. However, having influential friends did nothing to prevent his internment, and he found himself rubbing shoulders with the likes of Captain Schiffer, a senior Nazi police official and friend of Hitler. One man, who spoke no German and whose father had deserted his mother shortly after his birth, only learned of his German ancestry when they came to intern him.

Only a week before the outbreak of war, the government sub-committee responsible for the process belatedly realised that they would need separate camps for the pro-Nazis and the Jewish and other refugees. In consequence, these were not prepared in time. In some cases refugees were forced to endure the threats, abuse and violence of their Nazi fellow inmates for anything up to a year. The latter would jeer at the Jewish refugees' attempts to continue with their religious devotions, and would gather outside the accommodation of the Jews and refugees and lull them to sleep with the heart-warming sentiments of songs such as 'Wenn das Juden blut vom messer spritzt': 'When the blood of the Jews gushes forth from our knives, then everything goes twice as well.' Requests for segregation by the refugees themselves were repeatedly ignored by the authorities, as were anti-Jewish signs erected by the Nazis.

The process was conducted in a harsh and bureaucratic manner, given that many of these people had already suffered grievously in their home country. Families were split up, either as a consequence of being in different categories or because they were simply in different places at the time of arrest. They might even find themselves deported overseas without notice.

SWISS MOVEMENT

Perhaps the most extreme and, in some respects, most ludicrous example of innocents caught up in the British policy towards aliens concerned two Swiss men. Named Eggler and Schmid, they were working in Belgium when the Germans invaded and they tried to cycle back to Switzerland. They were arrested as possible paratroops by the French, on the not particularly persuasive grounds that one of them was carrying a rucksack. They were handed over to the British, with whom they were made to travel, via the beaches of Dunkirk, to Dover, where they were promptly refused entry to Britain. Given that arrangements for returning people to the continent were, at that time, not entirely straightforward, they were then interned. It took a month for the Swiss authorities to find them and six to get them released to neutral Portugal.

The random nature of the process is illustrated by the case of a ten-year-old German Jewish boy, who was being sponsored by a British barrister to attend school at Winchester. But Winchester was in a prohibited area, and under the new restrictions an alien could not live there. Had the barrister chosen almost any other public school, the problem would not have arisen. However, before he could arrange for the boy's transfer, he had been interned and deported to Canada.

In another case a British woman had married a Category C German – a man whose loyalty to Britain was unquestioned. She was told that she could reclaim her British nationality within two months. Due to some bureaucratic muddle, this was not done and, when the new regulations came in, her husband was immediately arrested and she herself was declared an enemy alien. Others, who actually wanted to go overseas – who were in transit through Britain en route to some third country – were also caught up in the process and arrested.

As the numbers of interned aliens increased rapidly, the authorities were overwhelmed and forced to use the most unsuitable accommodation for them. An unfinished housing estate at Huyton, near Liverpool, was requisitioned and surrounded by high barbed-wire fences. Twelve men were placed in each part-completed house with no furniture and just a sackful of straw each for a mattress. Others initially slept in tents beside the houses. Due to the shortage of coal for heating, they were allowed only one bath a month – which was perhaps just as well, since there was also a severe shortage of soap, towels and other basic materials. All cooking and eating had to be done in tents, whatever the weather.

Further investigation revealed that about a third of those interned on the estate were unfit to endure such treatment – the police had largely ignored Home Office instructions not to arrest the invalid or infirm. About 40 per cent of the inmates were found to be over 50 years of age, and many of them were considerably older. One house was completely filled with advanced tuberculosis cases. A single doctor, woefully short of medical supplies, served all the four thousand people living on the estate, assisted by whatever medical help the other inmates could provide. They were denied books, newspapers and wirelesses. Letters were delayed and censored.

Even worse conditions were faced by those housed in Warth Mills, a disused cotton mill in Bury. The floors where they slept were covered in cotton waste, oil and grease. The only light came through the glass roof, which was broken in many places, letting in the rain. Five hundred men shared eighteen cold water taps and filthy toilets, and they were half-starved – their evening meal consisting of a lump of bread, a small piece of cheese and a cup of tea. Few of the inmates had mattresses; most had to make do with a couple of (often verminous) blankets, and they shared this salubrious accommodation with rats. The Red Cross visited the site and complained about the conditions, as did Sir Walter Monckton from the Ministry of Information, who wrote: 'The two men who succeeded in committing suicide had already been in Hitler's concentration camps. Against these they held out, but this camp has broken their spirit.'

Others found themselves in tented camps or deported to the Isle of Man, where they became a poor substitute for the peacetime tourist trade. In Onchan camp they lived in grossly overcrowded conditions, two to a bed with others sleeping on the floors between the beds. No radios and, initially, no newspapers were allowed, and mail was delayed in a monstrous backlog of censorship that at one time reached a hundred thousand letters. A survey of those at Onchan gave some indication of the threat this group of evacuees posed to British security. Of the 1,491 inmates, 121 were artists or men of letters, 113 scientists or teachers, 68 lawyers, and 67 engineers; 1,230 of them were Jewish; 148 were married to British women, and no fewer than 1,080 of them had attempted to sign up in the British armed forces, to fight the Germans.

But even these spartan conditions were considered over-generous by the anti-alien lobby. It was claimed in the press that the prisoners on the Isle of Man were living in the lap of luxury, with private golf courses, beaches, cinema shows, the benefits of sea air and, of course, full hotel catering. Even the camp at Huyton was regarded as if it offered preferential treatment of some kind, with complaints voiced in Parliament about the aliens getting new homes while Britons continued to live in slums.

> MISSING CHILDREN
>
> 'In the summer of 1939 my father sent us to Shottery near Stratford. My brother and I caught chickenpox. We were looked after by a German-Jewish doctor. He taught us how to make animals in plasticine – lions, elephants, horses and camels. He drew ink circles round the last pock marks on our arms and legs. We asked him where his children were. He cried. I asked my mother why he had cried. 'Don't ask so many questions!' she said. 'He cried!' said my brother. Then my mother cried. We were totally baffled.
>
> Girl aged six, London, quoted in Westall.

By a further irony, the Nazis who were interned enjoyed substantially better conditions, for a number of reasons. First, they had greater protection under the Geneva Convention, whereas the British could virtually make up their own rules for 'friendly' aliens. Secondly, the British government was afraid that, if they were harsh on Nazi internees, the German authorities might take retaliatory action against those British nationals interned in Germany. More sinister was the suggestion that some of those responsible for their captivity felt greater sympathy for their Nazi inmates, as people who somehow 'stuck to their principles' in adversity (regardless of how distasteful those principles may be).

Swanwick, the first camp set up exclusively for interned Nazis, was a spacious manor house in Derbyshire, set in extensive grounds. All the older Nazis had their own rooms, with central heating and good plumbing. Moreover, the inmates effectively ran the place, with their own processes of censorship and discipline.

By the end of June 1940 the total number interned had reached 27,200. The Dominions were eventually persuaded to take substantial numbers of them, because it was felt that they constituted a major security risk if they remained in Britain. Over 11,000 internees were eventually shipped out. For many, the journeys to Canada or Australia proved hellish – and for a considerable number, they were to prove fatal.

Unlike the prisoners who were transported to the colonies in the nineteenth century, the internees were not even told where they were going. Some, as they were marched, at bayonet point, to the docks in Liverpool by soldiers, were pelted with rubbish by angry crowds. At the dockside, many had their valuables stolen or thrown into the sea. Those who managed to hold on to their possessions subsequently had them stolen by the crews on the ships or by their Canadian guards on their arrival.

They were packed on to the ships at twice or more their peacetime capacity. Even on board ship the discrimination continued, with the German army personnel getting the first claim on the cabins and the refugees often kept virtually imprisoned below decks throughout the voyage. Lynton describes a hellish crossing to Canada, during which an epidemic of dysentery broke out. Those who escaped the disease spent five solid days working naked in the sweltering heat below decks to clear up with their bare hands the mess left by the victims.

Throughout, their treatment seems to have been based upon the assumption that they were all virulent Nazis, which was far from the truth. A group of refugee monks found themselves jeered as they disembarked, in the belief that they were disguised Nazi paratroopers who had not yet had time to change out of their fancy dress since dropping on Holland! The Canadians, on receiving a bunch of supposedly desperate Nazi criminals, were surprised to find themselves controlling groups of callow schoolboys and left-wing sailors, about a third of whom demanded kosher food.

The cruellest fate awaited the men who left Liverpool on 1 July on board the *Arandora Star*. One day out from England, she was torpedoed and sank with the loss of 650 lives. The ship's normal peacetime capacity was 700 and there were lifeboats on board for 1,000 people (but not all of them proved capable of being launched). But for this voyage, the ship was packed with 1,564 people. No lifeboat drill had been explained to the passengers, many of whom were elderly and infirm.

Despite the death toll, the British press continued to attack the internees. According to the *Daily Express*:

> Soldiers and sailors . . . told of the panic among the aliens when they realised the ship was sinking. All condemned the cowardice of the Germans, who fought madly to get into the boats. 'The Germans were fighting with the Italians to escape, they were great hulking brutes', said one soldier. 'They punched and kicked their way past the Italians. We had to restrain them forcibly.' . . . 'But the Italians were just as bad. The whole mob of them thought of their own skins first. The scramble for the boats was sickening.'

Subsequent investigations showed this account to be entirely false. Just to complete the inglorious tale, Anthony Eden further tried to blacken their memory by claiming in the House of Commons that all the passengers on the *Arandora Star* were either Italian Fascists or Category A Germans, and that none were refugees. He was reminded of the names of some of the prominent anti-Nazis who had gone down with the ship and duly promised to re-check his facts. He would not have been helped by the fact that the paperwork surrounding the departure of the ship had been in chaos, and nobody was sure precisely who was on it. Government inquiries were eventually launched, both into the deaths on the *Arandora Star* and into conditions at the Huyton internment camp.

The *Arandora Star* episode marked the beginning of the end of mass internment. The excesses of the press had begun to turn public opinion against internment. Many of the great and the good in the arts and literature, in particular, began to campaign against it, as much for the ham-fisted way in which it had been put into practice as for the basic principle. The anti-internment case began to get more of a hearing in the mainstream press. Michael Foot was able to write in the *Evening Standard* on 17 July 1940:

> If we intern German anti-Nazis who fought Hitler for years, why not also intern De Gaulle? This war is not about national frontiers; it is on a scale not seen since the Reformation. Instead of interning German political refugees we should use them as speakers to reach the hearts and minds of Germans and as underground fighters to spark off a revolution.

Public opinion shifted rapidly. Between mid-July and early August 1940 the proportion of the public in favour of wholesale internment fell from 55 per cent to about 30 per cent. In August Winston Churchill, once one of the most ardent 'internists' in the Cabinet, told the Commons, without a hint of irony or embarrassment, that he had always thought the 'Fifth Column danger somewhat exaggerated in this Island'. Sir John Anderson spoke more candidly to the Commons on 22 August:

> I am not going to deny for a moment that the most regrettable and deplorable things have happened. . . . They have been due partly to the inevitable haste with which the policy of internment, once decided upon, had to be carried out. They have been due in some cases to the mistakes of individuals and to stupidity and muddle. These matters all relate to the past. So far as we can remedy mistakes, we shall remedy them.

During a parliamentary debate shortly before that, the government admitted that it knew of only one case (details unspecified) of a serious hostile act committed by an alien. Category C internees began to be released in significant numbers on 5 August. By the end of the month about a thousand had been set free, and by the end of the year almost nine thousand. Releases continued at about a thousand a month into 1941.

The Foreign Office belatedly set up a committee to advise on the welfare of internees and 'measures for maintaining the morale of aliens in this country so as to bind them more closely to our common cause'. Behind the scenes, the Foreign Office also launched a vicious attack on the ineptitude of MI5's part in the process, forcing an apology from the Chairman of the Joint Intelligence Committee.

The whole process had not only caused great hardship and injustice, and bureaucratic chaos, but had diverted significant resources away from any useful contribution to the war effort, and had denied the nation the efforts of a substantial and, for the vast majority, devotedly anti-Nazi group of people. For some, already burdened by the suffering they had undergone in their native country, anxieties about the safety of the families they had left behind and other factors, this treatment was the last straw.

The suicides in Warth Mills had succeeded in their grim mission. Another, 23-year-old Katherina Schwind, a domestic servant of Austrian descent, was found trying to gas herself. Her employer promptly moved her on to a couch and called not an ambulance, but the police. She was charged with attempted suicide and bound over to keep the peace (and, presumably, to stay alive) for twelve months.

Hitler, speaking at a Fuhrer Conference in July 1940, admitted: 'We cannot count that there would be much support at our disposal in England.' He found this out the hard way. Attempts to win over disaffected Welsh and Scottish Nationalists proved unsuccessful, and even the German contacts with the IRA in Dublin ended when the Irish government expelled the Germans' liaison officer.

In the absence of a spy network, much of the German intelligence about Britain and most of the European countries they conquered came from maps and guides that could be purchased in Berlin before the war. Studies of German intelligence sources after the war revealed the paucity and often inaccuracy of the information they possessed about Britain. Indeed, research carried out for UNESCO after the war indicated that, throughout western Europe, the idea of a Fifth Column on any significant scale had been a myth. Norwegian minefields 'defused' by Fifth Columnists had never been laid. Dutch bridges were not left undestroyed because of sabotage, but because the Dutch troops guarding them, expecting French reinforcements, had neglected to place any charges underneath them. False orders were never given.

One unexpected positive result of this whole unhappy process came from the fact that foreign nationals were not allowed to work on projects with direct application to the war effort. However, the more 'pure science' of atomic energy was not at that time covered by this war work rule, so a number of them went on to work on the Manhattan Project – which led in turn to the nuclear bomb and to the shortening of the war against Japan.

## ANTI-ALIEN FEELING AMONG THE GENERAL PUBLIC

Anti-alien feeling may not have been widespread before the newspaper campaigns got to work, but it soon found fertile soil in which to grow. It was not always well directed. Many employers summarily dismissed their Hungarian staff on the outbreak of war, notwithstanding the fact that Hungary was a neutral country. They did not even meet their legal obligations to pay them wages in lieu of notice or their fare home, with the result that large numbers descended on the Hungarian Legation, looking for help. Seventeen 'enemy aliens' engaged in ARP work in Marylebone were sacked in May 1940 and the London County Council dismissed all Germans in its employ in early June.

Discrimination affected even the most long-standing and unimpeachable resident. This case was reported in the *Maidenhead Advertiser* in July 1940:

> A petition, signed by some five hundred persons, has been forwarded to the Ministry of Home Security in regard to the continuance in office as Head A.R.P. Warden of Mr M.J. Speer, whose surname was formerly Mecklenburg. The view was expressed in the petition that it is wrong to permit persons of enemy origin or connection to occupy key positions in civil defence . . . to restore public confidence in the integrity and efficiency of our local civil defence services, we ask that . . . they appoint in Mr Speer's place a person without enemy taint.

And what was Mr Speer's dangerously subversive background? He had been born in Middlesex in 1883, his father having been a naturalised Englishman at the time of his marriage. The only time he had left his native shores was to fight the Germans during the First World War, where he distinguished himself by winning three medals and rising to the rank of staff sergeant. Mr Speer not unnaturally put the petition down to the activities of Fifth Columnists.

Following the outbreak of war, refugees continued to arrive in Britain at a rate of around 800 per month, until about 150,000 were living here. Only about a third of them were Jewish, but the blanket term 'refu-jew' was insultingly applied to them all, initially by the British Union of Fascists. Anti-Semitism grew during the war years. A survey in 1940 showed that 17 per cent of the population even agreed with Lord Haw-Haw's proposition that the Allies were fighting the war on behalf of Jews and

---

ANTI-SEMITISM

I was travelling on the Tube to Edgware and people were getting up, making speeches. 'It's about time we caved in to Hitler. When all's said and done he's doing a good job, he's murdering all these bloody Jews.' They were probably Fascists.

Commercial traveller, quoted by Grafton.

capitalists. This Home Intelligence report from 6 May 1943 illustrates the problem:

> During the last three weeks comment about Jews in this country appears to have increased slightly. Jews continue to be criticised for black marketing, escaping the call-up and 'displaying ostentatious wealth'. In London, the North Midland and North Western regions, there is said to be an increase in anti-semitism – 'the spreading of which is seemingly in some cases deliberately organised and fostered'; it is suggested that, in Hornsey, 'anti-semitism due to ignorance and prejudice is exploited by Fascist elements'. Reference is also made to 'undue prominence shown in the press to court cases against Jews'.

This anti-Semitism was despite public knowledge beginning to emerge of Hitler's ill-treatment of them in continental Europe. At first, the Ministry of Information had been unwilling to publish the information about the concentration camps, because of the anti-Semitism in the country at large. Details of the appalling toll of lives were received from the middle of 1942, but it was not until 17 December that Anthony Eden announced them to the House of Commons. When he did, cynicism about the false German atrocity stories circulated during the First World War led a good number of the general public to disbelieve them.

Relationships between Jews and the rest of the population were complex. While those who were either positively pro-Jewish or actively anti-Semitic were both in a minority, opinion research suggests that a sizeable part of the population held views about Jews that were to varying degrees ambivalent. Mass Observation found evidence of anti-Semitism to some degree among more than 55 per cent of one of its survey populations.

What is clear is that anti-Semitism was much more institutionalised and respectable than it is today. People apparently found it easy to separate their anti-Semitism from their opposition to Nazism. A Mass Observation survey in January 1944 found 24 per cent of the population calling for stricter controls over the activities of British Fascists, while only 2 per cent of the same population saw the need for any curbs on anti-Semitism. Clubs and societies commonly had an open policy of excluding Jews, and A.J.P. Taylor has suggested that many people were 'annoyed at having to repudiate the anti-Semitism which they had secretly cherished', as a result of the Nazis' persecution of the Jews. A best-selling author like Douglas Reed could use openly and quite extremely anti-Semitic themes in his books – for example, *Insanity Fair*, published in 1938, had the Jews taking over London. Despite being forced by his publisher to tone down some of his worst excesses, Reed still attracted much criticism – as well as a huge readership – for fiction that was as racist as it was racy. He ended the war as foreign editor for Kemsley newspapers, despite being associated with some extreme anti-Semitic organisations.

He was far from alone. Another bestselling author, Warwick Deeping, featured crude caricatures of Jews in his 1941 book *The Dark House*, in which popular detective Sexton Blake pitted his wits against a 'Jewish financier' (the stereotype was so well established that it hardly needed further elaboration) who controlled both the Bank of England and the Bank of China. Improbably, Jewish characters even found their way into fiction as leading lights in the Gestapo. On the radio, a series of plays called *Born to be King*, broadcast in 1941–2 and written by Dorothy L. Sayers, portrayed the Jews of biblical times in such a hostile light that it led to complaints from the Jewish community, and to Jewish children being bullied at school for 'killing Jesus'. The BBC's response was to repeat the series over Easter 1943. This was a lapse from a generally creditable record on anti-Semitism by the BBC during the war years.

Anti-Semitism was not restricted to one part of the political spectrum. While it found its most virulent voice on the extreme right, mainstream Conservatives also displayed it to various degrees. Churchill himself had been a leading protagonist of the existence of a Jewish/Communist conspiracy in 1918, but now advised others in the party to 'be careful, whatever the temptation, not to be drawn into any campaign that might be represented as anti-Semitic'.

None the less a group of Conservative MPs lobbied against giving any refugees British nationality, since it would 'result in a permanent increase of our already over-large Jewish population . . . which was . . . a most unhealthy symptom in the body politic. The Jewish vote is so strong in some constituencies that the Member has no freedom of action.'

Not a single Jewish Conservative MP was elected in 1945. Even Lord Gort, who as High Commissioner for Palestine might have been expected to know better, was taken to task for making anti-Semitic remarks, but the complaints against him led to no disciplinary action from the government.

But anti-Semitism was also to be found on the radical left, where the Independent Labour Party attacked Jewish capitalism, among other things for causing the war. The ILP shared its anti-war position with the British Union of Fascists (BUF), and there had even been talk of a coalition between them in early 1939. The *Daily Worker* managed to condemn both anti-Semitism and Jewish financiers at the same time. Even after the liberation of the concentration camps there were those on the radical left who still believed that their main victims had been members of the German working classes.

The liberal centre opposed what it saw as Jewish exclusivity, and argued that the solution to prejudice was for them to become assimilated (that is, to give up their religion and their separate identity). Finally, well-meaning pacifist bodies such as the Peace Pledge Union were infiltrated by right-wing extremists, and their *Peace News* was given over to anti-Semitic attacks from the likes of the Duke of Bedford and the British National Party founder Edward Godfrey.

Among the lunatic fringes, wild views were held about Jewish plans for world domination. By 1943 some 70–80 per cent of German broadcasting time was given over to anti-Semitic material, including widespread publicity for the *Protocols of the Elders of Zion*. This told of a plot, dating from the time of King Solomon (and thus rather a long time in its gestation) for the Jews to overthrow Christianity and take over the world. Two editions of the *Protocols* were published and widely distributed during the war years. Running parallel to this was the school of thought that the present-day Jews were a mongrelised version of their biblical selves, and that the British were in fact the true descendants of God's chosen people.

The East End of London had one of the largest Jewish populations in Britain, and the fascists saw this area as their natural territory. If active anti-Semitism on a large scale was going to take root anywhere, it was likely to be here. In the event, the record of race relations there was patchy. In some cases, Jews and gentiles worked together to pursue common aims (as when the Stepney Tenants' Defence League successfully took on the slum landlords). In other areas, such as the Pembury Estate in Hackney, violence and attacks on Jewish property were used by the non-Jewish tenants in pursuit of a localised policy of ethnic cleansing. They were supported in this by the right-wing local newspaper, the *Hackney Gazette*. In more genteel areas of north-west London, similar sentiments took the form of a petition campaign, designed to remove aliens from the area.

Jews were prominent in the Civil Defence in the East End and, despite some initial tensions, appear generally to have worked well with their non-Jewish colleagues during the blitz. In the Tilbury shelter, Jews and gentiles united to persecute the local Indian population. Jewish shops were attacked in retaliation for the internment of leading fascists, and on one occasion, when a film at a Stepney cinema showed the Nazi persecution of the Jews, a racist element in the audience cheered, leading to a fight among the audience. But on the whole, the worst predictions of a breakdown in relations between the communities following bombing were not realised. Active anti-Semitism did not take root there on any large scale.

In the wider community, claims were commonly made that able-bodied Jews were displacing women and children in air raid shelters (something which George Orwell investigated and found to be groundless). The worst example of this occurred in March 1943 when 173 people were killed in front of Bethnal Green tube station. Some attempted to blame this disaster on panic among the local Jewish population. In fact, this was the non-Jewish part of the East End, the real heartland of the BUF, and the fact that only 3 per cent of those killed in the disaster were Jewish belies the rumour.

Jews were particularly accused of involvement in the black market. They were not helped in this by their strong association with consumer industries like food and clothing, where it was easy for a customer denied service by a genuine shortage to blame it on a Jewish conspiracy. Sections of the press seized upon these feelings. This is from the Janus column in the *Spectator*: 'There can be no doubt that a section, and a substantial section, of the Jewish community has a black record in this respect. It is not to anyone's advantage to keep complete silence in this matter.' Even normally sympathetic sources, like Cassandra in the *Daily Mirror*, echoed the concern: 'I have been examining the records of convictions for food misdemeanours, and it is impossible not to be struck by the number of Jewish offenders. Names like Blum, Cohen, Gold and the like occur with remarkable frequency.'

An analysis of black market prosecutions for the period April 1942 to May 1943 showed that, of more than 2,500 prosecutions, 10.9 per cent involved Jewish offenders. However, when this is compared to the proportion of businesses in Jewish ownership at the time, it appears that Jewish entrepreneurs were no worse (albeit no better) than their Aryan counterparts. The government did not publish these findings at the time, for fear of it being seen as Jewish propaganda. There is also some evidence that the newspapers were selective in the cases they publicised. For example, *The Grocer* in March 1942 reported forty-eight black market cases, only three of which involved Jews. However, it was these three cases that received some of the most extensive publicity in the wider press.

The Jewish community in Britain was, not surprisingly, sensitive to this current of opinion. In his 1943 Passover letter, the Chief Rabbi Dr J.H. Hertz warned: 'Though others are guilty of the same and even greater transgressions, they do not, in the eyes of the public, compromise their religious communities. But every Jew holds the good name of his entire people in his hand.'

The Jewish community, and its supporters such as the National Council for Civil Liberties, was active in trying to rebut anti-Semitic propaganda from whatever source (though the NCCL was simultaneously opposing Regulation 18B, which put the main peddlers of anti-Semitism behind bars, on the grounds of *habeas corpus*). How successful they all were is open to question, since their approach assumed that the holder of anti-Semitic views was susceptible to rational argument. They set up their own tribunal, to investigate the substance of the complaints being made against the community, but even this was turned against them by anti-Semites, who claimed that it was a device to by-pass established courts.

The Board of Jewish Deputies employed a public relations officer, whose main job was to go around London, correcting the behaviour of refugees – preventing them from speaking German too loudly, or warning Jewish restaurateurs against displaying German-language newspapers too openly in their premises.

The complaints against Jews were only silenced when the gates of Auschwitz and Belsen were opened to a horrified world.

## RACIAL PREJUDICE

People cheerful and optimistic at weekend when Hitler failed to invade Britain on Friday as threatened. General feeling now that war will last a long time, as invasion cannot succeed and we shall then settle down to hammering away at Germany by RAF. . . . Most coloured people reported anxious to pull weight in war effort; unable to, except in St Pancras where twenty are Air Raid wardens. Some dismissals because of colour.

Home Intelligence report 22 July 1940.

Many British citizens had scarcely seen a black person before the arrival of the GIs in 1942. To them, this strange breed might as well have come from the moon. Their exotic nature is illustrated by the fact that some of them were successful in persuading the gullible locals that their skin had been artificially blackened for camouflage in night exercises, and that an injection would restore them to white on their return home.

Many of the problems stemmed from the fact that the American Army was far more racist than the host population. Most American states still practised their own form of apartheid. Among the white GIs, there were plenty who would not drink out of a glass previously used by a black person, and British branches of the Ku Klux Klan were not uncommon.

> Colonel Blimp explains:
> 'Gad sir, Lucy Houston is right! Those black troops are fine patriotic fellows – so long as they don't forget themselves and try to fight for their own country.'

The subservience of many black GIs, born of years of discrimination and disadvantage in their own country, was taken by many Britons as politeness, as Home Intelligence reported in June 1944:

Coloured troops . . . are praised. In some cases they are said to be better behaved and 'less sloppy' than the whites; also, in the Huddersfield area, better behaved than the British troops.

People deplore the association of coloured troops with white girls, but it is the latter who are censured. At the same time, it is suggested that the negroes might be provided with a contingent of coloured Auxiliaries, or more camp amenities so that they should spend less time out.

There is some concern at the relations between white and coloured troops and at reports of friction between them. Recent cases of coloured men being condemned to death for rape have aroused strong local protests on grounds of colour discrimination (S.W. Region). In Norwich there is resentment that certain restaurants will not serve negroes.

A Home Office Circular of 1943 warned that: 'Some British women appear to find a particular fascination in association with men of colour. The morale of British troops is likely to be upset by rumours that their wives and daughters are being debauched by coloured American troops.'

But the danger was not just in one direction. In May 1944 a black GI was sentenced to death for the alleged rape of a white woman. The *Daily Mirror* took up his cause, exposing inconsistencies in the woman's case. They produced evidence that the woman had been operating as a prostitute and had 'promised to make trouble for him' when he jibbed at a doubling of her usual rates. Faced by a petition from thirty thousand readers, General Eisenhower set aside the conviction for lack of evidence.

Some of the British also practised their own colour bar. After being bombed out in June 1941, Sir Hari Singh Gour, a British citizen, Vice-Chancellor of Nagpur University and a distinguished Indian legal authority, was refused accommodation at the Caernarvon Hotel because he was coloured – one of many such cases. Leary Constantine, the famous cricketer and a British government employee, suffered a similar fate at the Imperial Hotel while captain of the West Indies cricket team. Amelia King, a third-generation British black woman, was refused enlistment in the Women's Land Army on grounds of colour. The Colonial Office pressed the Home Secretary in the light of the Singh case for legislation making clear the common law obligation on innkeepers and others to serve travellers of all colours.

> Colonel Blimp (as *maître d'hôtel*) explains:
> 'Gad sir! We can't have a coloured man here! It would take the minds of resident stinkers off their struggles for the ideals of the British family of free and equal peoples.'

About twelve thousand black GIs had arrived in Britain by October 1942. A War Cabinet memorandum from that time spells out the pressures this caused:

The Secretary for Foreign Affairs . . . undertook, with the approval of the War Cabinet, to press the USA authorities to reduce the number sent, but I believe he has met with little success. We are thus left to face the various problems to which their presence gives rise.

The policy of the United States military authorities in dealing with their coloured troops in this country is based on the modus vivendi which has been developed in the United States in the course of time as the result of conditions obtaining in that country. Their policy . . . rests on the principle of an almost complete separation between white and coloured troops. . . .

This policy may perhaps be fairly described as the combination of equal rights and segregation practised in the Southern States and is not generally known to the population of this country, who with little experience of a colour problem at home are naturally inclined to make no distinction between the treatment of white and coloured troops and are apt to regard such distinctions as undemocratic.

The War Office is thus faced with two incompatible theories, the disregard of either of which may have serious consequences. On the one hand the average white American soldier does not understand the normal British attitude to the colour problem and his respect for this country may suffer if he sees British troops and British Women's Services drawing no distinction between white and coloured. . . . Moreover, the coloured troops themselves probably expect to be treated in this country as in the Unites States, and a markedly different treatment might well cause political difficulties in America at the end of the war. It must be added that from the point of view of the morale of our troops, whether in this country or overseas, it is most undesirable that there should be any unnecessary association between American coloured troops and British women.

These considerations suggest that the War Office attitude toward the American coloured troops should be based on the view of the American Army authorities. . . .

To sum up, I would ask the endorsement of the War Cabinet of the policy I propose to follow in the Army. . . .

(a) To make full use of the American administrative arrangements for the segregation of coloured troops, but where those fail to make no official segregation against them.

(b) To give the Army through ABCA [Army Bureau of Current Affairs] a knowledge of the history and facts of the colour question in the USA and the USA Army.

(c) To allow Army officers without the issue of overt or written instructions to interpret those facts to the personnel of the army including the ATS and so educate them to adopt towards the USA coloured troops the attitude of the USA Army Authorities.

Officially the British government said it would not assist the US Army in enforcing segregation, but the Cabinet agreed not to object to that policy and to caution Britons against becoming too friendly with black GIs. Secretary of State for War Sir James Grigg wanted to go further. He proposed a guidance note for British servicemen which talked about the white American southerner's moral duty to the negro 'as it were to a child'. It spoke patronisingly of the negro's 'simple mental outlook' and his lack of 'the white man's ability to think and act to a plan'. The War Cabinet backtracked from the position of educating the troops in the ways of racism, and made it clear that no segregation in British public facilities would take place. Stafford Cripps drew up instructions for British service personnel which included the following:

The coming of American negro troops to this country may place members of the Services in difficult situations owing to the differences of outlook between the white American personnel and the British personnel as to the relationship between black and white people.

It has therefore been thought advisable to issue the following instructions as to the advice that should be given to the British Service personnel in this matter. . . .

It is necessary, therefore, for British men and women to recognise the problem and take account of the attitude of the white American citizen. This will prevent any straining of our amicable relations with the US Army through misunderstanding which knowledge and forethought can prevent. . . .

2. British soldiers and auxiliaries should try to understand the American attitude to the relationship of white and coloured people, and to appreciate why it is different from the attitude of most people in this country who normally come into contact with only an occasional Negro. . . .

7. There is no reason why British soldiers and auxiliaries should adopt the American attitude but they should respect it and avoid making it a subject for argument and dispute. They must endeavour to understand the American point of view and they must always be on their guard against giving offence.

8. There is certain practical advice which should be given as follows:

(a) be friendly and sympathetic towards coloured American troops – but remember that in their own country they are not accustomed to close and intimate relationships with white people.

(b) if you find yourself in the company of white and coloured American troops (as for example if American troops come into a canteen or bar where you are in the company of coloured Americans), make it your business to avoid unpleasantness. It is much the best, however, to avoid such situations.

(c) for a white woman to go about in the company of a Negro American is likely to lead to controversy and ill-feeling; it may also be misunderstood by the Negro troops themselves. This does not mean that friendly hospitality in the home or in social gatherings need be ruled out, though in such cases care should be taken not to invite white and coloured American troops at the same time.

(d) avoid arguments over the colour question; but if it comes up in discussions with American troops listen patiently to what the Americans have to say and, without necessarily agreeing with them, make up your own mind that you will not allow it to become an occasion for ill-feeling or open dispute.

(e) be on your guard against ill-disposed people who are out to use the colour question as a means of stirring up trouble between Americans and ourselves.

One of the first serious outbreaks of racially motivated trouble came in Launceston, Cornwall, in September 1943, where black and white GIs fought over white women who were not observing the US Army's colour bar. The following year, there were race riots in Manchester, after a black sailor was seen kissing a white girl at a railway station. More serious still, black GIs were driven out of a pub in Kingsclere, near Newbury, by white colleagues. They returned, armed, and in the fight which followed the landlord's wife was shot dead.

Joan Pountney, a member of the Women's Land Army, describes another inter-racial fight in a pub:

'The pub was packed with soldiers, British and American. I was sitting with some land girls at one table. A group of black servicemen were at another over the other side of the pub. One of the black chaps had been very kind to a friend of mine, giving her lifts and so forth. The Americans started to sing – 'Bless 'em all' – and my friend said, 'I'm going to buy him a pint to say thank you'. She got half way over with the pint when a British paratroop sergeant walked over to her and knocked the glass out of her hand, saying that the Americans singing a British song was an insult. That was it. They smashed the place to pieces. The landlord rushed over and told us to leave through his quarters. 'If you get caught up in this I'll be in trouble with your people,' he said. There were a good many men walking around with black eyes the next day.

Recorded in Tyrer.

The black GIs left a more permanent memento of their time in Britain. It is estimated that there were some fifteen hundred mixed-race children in Britain at the end of the war. Most of their mothers could not join the army of post-war GI brides crossing the Atlantic, since mixed marriages were at that time still illegal in most American states.

# TWO

# THE EVACUEES

The evacuation could have done on a major scale what a tiny handful of charitable societies had been struggling to do for years – to give the children of the slums a chance of a fuller, freer life in the open country. It left, instead, a scar on the national consciousness, the majority of hosts and guests alike looking back on the experience with a profound dislike. Two contrasting sides of Britain had been brought into enforced contact with each other and neither much liked what it saw.

*E.R. Chamberlin,* Life in Wartime Britain

If race and nationality were divisive factors in wartime society, so too was the gulf between two sets of native Britons – the urban poor and rural England. As the last days of peace ebbed away in 1939, the government set in motion the largest mass movement of people ever seen in this country. Large parts of the population were to be removed from the nation's main towns and cities. From 7 a.m. on Friday nine key routes out of London became one-way streets, partly to assist those who were evacuating under their own steam. Normal bus and rail services were drastically curtailed or cancelled entirely, as three thousand special buses and four thousand trains were brought into operation by twelve thousand volunteer helpers. Passenger ferries were pressed into service to take some of the evacuees out of London by sea. Similar arrangements were being put into operation in provincial towns and cities, and news came from France that the people of Paris were also being moved out.

*The Times* reported that news of the evacuation had put a dampener on the stock market and that little trade had been done. They also gave an indication of the scale of the undertaking: 'By Monday evening, if all goes well, three million schoolchildren, mothers with infants, expectant mothers, invalids and blind persons will be in the safe reception areas with their temporary hosts.' It was, the paper emphasised, purely a precautionary measure which was bound in any case to take place before any international crisis had reached a final stage. They told their readers: 'No one should conclude that this decision means that war is now regarded as inevitable' – but few were by then willing to believe that this was the case.

## PLANNING FOR EVACUATION

The journey from school to the station by crocodiles of schoolchildren on 1 September went relatively smoothly – most of them had had a rehearsal three days previously. But the plans for evacuation went back a long way further than that, to the days immediately following the First World War. The Germans made 103 air raids on Britain during that war, killing over 1,400 people and injuring almost 4,000. In the worst attack, by just seventeen bombers in 1917, 162 people were killed and over 400 injured. While these losses were relatively small in the context of the deaths that took place in the trenches, they had a huge impact on the general public, who found themselves in the front line for the first time.

The fear of bombing was compounded after the war by a series of wildly exaggerated estimates of its potential effects. The sub-text to these over-estimates was the political battle being fought by the fledgeling Royal Air Force to retain its independence as the third armed force. The estimates of the consequences of bombing grew steadily more wild as war approached. The first error in the debate was the belief in the invulnerability of the bomber. As Stanley Baldwin put it to the House of Commons in 1932:

> I think it is as well for the man in the street to realise that there is no power on earth that can prevent him from being bombed. Whatever people may tell him, the bomber will always get through. The only defence is offence, which means you have to kill more women and children more quickly than the enemy if you want to save yourselves.

The second error related to the quantity of bombs an enemy was likely to drop. In 1924 it was assumed that the first twenty-four hours of any new war would see more than 300 tons of high explosive dropped on Britain – more than had been dropped in the whole of the First World War. By 1938 this estimate had risen to 100,000 tons of bombs in the first fourteen days of war. In the event Germany dropped a total 64,393 tons of bombs on Britain in the entire war. This was the equivalent of just 3 per cent of the bombs dropped by the Allies on Germany.

The likely impact of bombing was also wildly exaggerated. The official calculation as war approached was that every ton of bombs dropped would result in fifty casualties, a third of which would be fatal. This estimate was originally made by the Air Staff in 1924. But it was reinforced by the experience of Guernica, during the Spanish Civil War, where bombers attacked a defenceless village in daylight on a busy market day – hardly a reliable indicator of what would happen when Germany attacked England. By 1937 the Imperial Defence Committee was forecasting 1.8 million casualties, 600,000 of which would occur in the first two months, and a requirement for anything up to 2.8 million hospital beds. Insanity on a huge scale was also forecast, outnumbering physical casualties three to one. With forecasts like these, it was small wonder that the authorities concentrated on how they would bury the dead, rather than on meeting the needs of the survivors. It may also go some way to explaining Neville Chamberlain's unwillingness to confront Hitler.

Accordingly, during April 1939 the Ministry of Health very quietly issued a million burial forms to the local authorities, who in turn began stockpiling large supplies of coffins. These were made of papier mâché or stout cardboard, partly for ease of storage and partly because the authorities could not afford the £300,000-worth of coffin wood that they thought would be required in the first three months. In practice, bombing (including the V1s and V2s and long-range shelling) was to claim 60,595 lives during the entire war – the true figure was nearer to one than to fifty casualties per ton of bombs.

The final exaggeration related to the impact of bombing on civilian morale. Sir Hugh Trenchard, founding father of the Royal Air Force, told the Committee of Imperial Defence in 1923 that if people were subjected to enough bombing they would compel the government to sue for peace. J.F.C. Fuller, in the same year, put it rather more colourfully:

> Picture if you can what the results will be; London for a few days will be one vast raving Bedlam, the hospitals will be stormed, traffic will cease, the homeless will shriek for help, the City will be in Pandemonium. What of the Government in Westminster? It will be swept away by an avalanche of terror. The enemy will dictate his terms which will be grasped like a straw by a drowning man.

This was the context in which the idea of evacuation evolved. From as early as December 1924 plans began to be prepared to move much of the civilian population out of the cities in the event of war. At this time there was no thought of Germany being in a position to attack Britain – France was assumed to be the most likely aggressor.

The idea of the government evacuating every child from London was decided not to be feasible, and the idea grew up instead that they would evacuate only the poorest. There were several reasons for this; first, they lived in the areas most likely to be bombed; secondly, they would be less well able to evacuate themselves. But also underpinning this decision were concerns about public order and the sanctity of property. As one of the sub-committees overseeing the Air Raid Precautions in the 1930s put it, those most likely to panic would in their view be 'the less stable in character of foreign elements within London as well as the very poor in east and southern London'. These groups were identified as 'foreign, Jewish and poor elements' and it was claimed that these would turn out to be 'the classes of person most likely to be driven mad with fright'. Similar concerns lay behind the decision to carry out evacuation before hostilities actually started. This was done in order to prevent people bolting and thereby causing a panic in the streets that would undermine the morale of the country, making it difficult to control. It was also feared that, if London were bombed, 'the poor might flock back into the wealthier areas where they would find prizes worth having'. But the committee took pains to point out that 'any discrimination against the foreign element or the poor was there for the sake of the whole'.

Winston Churchill, speaking in a Commons debate in November 1934, gave his view of the likely scale of the disruption bombing would cause:

> We must expect that under pressure of continuous air attack upon London, at least 3 or 4,000,000 people will be driven out into the open country around the metropolis. This vast amount of human beings, far larger than any armies which have been fed and moved in war, without shelter and without food, without sanitation and without special provision for the maintenance of order, would confront the government of the day with an administrative problem of the first magnitude, and would certainly absorb the energies of our small army and our territorial force.

The plan for evacuation in the event of war was first made public in 1933. But the detailed organisation of it was left until much later. In January 1938 the Board of Education shifted responsibility on to local authorities for preparing evacuation schemes, but the confusion that this lack of central direction caused led them to withdraw that decision two months later. Councils were told not to draw up schemes until instructed to do so by the Home Secretary. The government finally set up the Anderson Committee to draw up evacuation plans in May 1938, but their recommendations were not approved by Parliament until the end of October 1938 – just ten months before the outbreak of war. By that time there had already been an unofficial mini-evacuation in September 1938, at the time of the Munich crisis. When the Anderson Committee handed over responsibility for implementing the scheme to the Department of Health, the Imperial Defence Committee was told: 'Evacuation plans are, at present, very backward.'

The evacuation plans were developed very much in secret. As a result, very little account was taken of the views of those whose cooperation would be vital to their success – the authorities in both the evacuating and the receiving areas, and the evacuee families themselves. Many of the mistakes that were made might at least have been identified, if not necessarily overcome, by obtaining those views. The authorities also took for granted the unquestioning cooperation of the teaching staff involved and failed to provide any expert monitoring of the billeting arrangements – this again being left to the teachers. Furthermore, the Anderson Committee failed to anticipate the hostility of working-class parents to the idea of sending their children to live with strangers. As a study for the Fabian Society in 1940 put it:

Surely only male calculations could have so confidently assumed that working-class wives would be content to leave their husbands indefinitely to look after themselves, and only middle-class parents, accustomed to shooing their children out of sight and reach at the earliest possible age, could have been so astonished to find that working-class parents were violently unwilling to part with theirs.

This unwillingness of inner-city people to part with their children produced one of the first cracks in the exercise. Only about a third of the expected number initially took up the offer of evacuation. This led to a radical telescoping of the departure times of trains that caused chaos in some of the reception areas. In some places, they waited for hours for trains that did not arrive, or arrived with many fewer, or different kinds of, evacuees than those expected. The arrangements in the reception areas were in any event relatively *ad hoc*, since local authorities were only given permission to spend anything on them three days before the exercise began.

> Colonel Blimp explains: 'Gad sir! Colonel Pitt-Drivels is right! This billeting of children idea is damned nonsense. The poorer classes must be lacking in decent family instinct not to want their brats blown up with them.'

The Anderson Committee had previously designated authorities as 'evacuation areas', 'neutral areas' or 'reception areas', according to the danger they were thought to face of being bombed. With the benefit of hindsight, the committee's designation of areas looks questionable in some cases. For example, Bristol, Plymouth and Nottingham were all defined as neutral areas, not to be evacuated – with what proved to be serious consequences for those populations.

This was compounded in some cases by a confusion as to which authorities were to receive evacuees and which send them. It emerged that Essex authorities along the Thames Estuary were preparing to send their children away from what they thought might become a battle zone, at the same time as London authorities were preparing to evacuate some of their children to the relative 'safety' of these same areas. In some cases the final destination of the evacuees was a matter of pure chance. One group of schoolchildren from West Ham were scheduled to move to Somerset, but caused a near-riot on their non-corridor train when the driver failed to stop to allow them a toilet break. This forced the driver to make an unscheduled halt at Wantage, and it was here that the West Ham boys ended up spending their war years.

Billeting officers none the less made heroic efforts to place the new arrivals, though the process for doing so was variously likened to a Roman slave auction or a cattle market. Older, fitter boys and girls were more readily snapped up as potential farm or domestic labour. More appealing-looking children were chosen for their aesthetic value, while the less winsome, those with disfiguring diseases and those who stubbornly refused to be separated from one or more siblings proved to be far more difficult to place. Exhausted children would find themselves left in an ever-dwindling band of human 'remnants', pored over by unenthusiastic would-be hosts, and finally hawked from door to door with only the Billeting Officer's threat of compulsion securing some of them a lodging. Some were unplaceable even then; in Maidenhead, as no doubt in many other areas, a special home had to be set up for 'unbilletable boys', where they were given 'a course of correctional treatment under Mrs Porter, the Matron'. In the desperate effort to secure a roof – any roof – over their heads, no thought could be given to trying to match the backgrounds of host and evacuee.

All this differed markedly from the rosy picture presented of the evacuation in the press:

> The reception in various districts of the evacuated schoolchildren was carried out with the same efficiency that characterised the departures. Competent nurses and reception officers saw that each child got milk and food before being taken to the billeting centres, from where the children were conducted to their temporary homes.
> There was no confusion, the teachers who were in charge of the children paid close attention to the details of the arrangements that had been made beforehand. . . . So far no casualties have been reported. . . . For all but a few, it was an enthralling but happy adventure, and homesickness and shyness quickly fled at the sight of new faces, new surroundings and new playmates. . . . Some of them were soon eating high teas beyond their dreams and many went up later to bedrooms larger and airier than they had thought possible.

This was far from the picture painted by many members of the public. The Oxford academic R.C.K. Ensor kicked off what turned into a near-hate campaign in the *Spectator*: his article described the evacuees as follows: 'Many of the new arrivals were the lowest grade of slum women – slatternly malodorous tatterdemalions trailing children to match.' Others wrote to the publication in similar vein, one contributor (using the pseudonym 'A Victim') calling the *Spectator*: 'the only paper which has broken the careful conspiracy of lies, organised on the Nazi model, to blanket the hardships inflicted on the victims in the "safe" areas', and going on to complain of the authorities 'thrusting filthy women and children into the homes of decent cleanly [sic] people, who then had to give up their jobs to care full-time for a couple of evacuees for the princely sum of 17s per week.' Another anonymous contributor said: 'When I read the Ministry of Health's unctuous and self-satisfied congratulations on the success of the scheme, I can only wish some official of that Ministry had been present here at our reception.'

The enforced timing of the first evacuation – right at the end of the school summer holiday – brought additional problems. First, it was the height of the head-lice season, since several weeks away from the ministrations of the school 'nit nurse' had produced increased numbers of cases. This was compounded by the children's close proximity to each other on the long train journeys, creating infestations of epidemic proportions. It was estimated that London evacuees had about a 35 per cent incidence of head-lice, and one Medical Officer of Health in an area receiving Liverpudlian evacuees ordered all the new arrivals' heads to be shaved, when 50 per cent infestation rates began to appear. Some hosts in rural areas were alleged to have used sheep dip as an extreme cure for their guests' unwanted vermin. (There were at this time unfounded fears among the general public that head-lice could lead to the spread of typhus.)

Health officers were appointed to examine the evacuees on arrival, though the thoroughness of that examination may be judged from the fact that, during the second (1940) evacuation, they were supposed to check 480 children per hour. Rudimentary checks for lice and scabies were all that were possible, and any evidence this revealed of other potential problems was referred to a proper doctor for a closer look. There was good reason to expect that the general state of health of the evacuees would leave a great deal to be desired in other respects. Just before the war, in 1937, a survey of London schoolchildren had revealed that 67–70 per cent had bone disorders, 67–83 per cent had enlarged or septic tonsils and 88–93 per cent had malformed or decaying teeth. A quarter of them were deemed to be malnourished. At this time public school pupils were on average four inches taller than the rest of the school population, largely on account of their superior diet.

The timing of the evacuation also meant that many of the children had not yet been given their new clothes at the start of the school year – impoverished parents would have left their purchase to the last minute. It had also been a long, hot summer, so many of them would have travelled to their new homes with a very limited and particularly worn-out wardrobe. This problem was exacerbated by the evacuating authorities, which encouraged mothers not to pack too many clothes for their offspring, in an effort to cut down the amount of luggage to be carried.

Nor were the receiving local authorities encouraged to spend money on clothes for any new arrivals found to be lacking them, on the very reasonable grounds that everybody would then want some. They were authorised to spend just £1 per 200 children on the most extreme cases (and to do this without giving any publicity to their having done so), with the result that the burden often fell on the foster parent. For those who took up the burden of hosting an evacuee, the 10*s* per week allowance (8*s* 6*d* each if you took more than one child) was certainly not sufficient to reimburse the cost of clothing. Others just left their new guests to shiver.

Other shortcomings in the wardrobe department were the product of ignorance or grinding poverty. Little girls were found to possess no knickers; children were strangers to the concept of pyjamas, while one Scottish housewife found her new guests unwilling to climb between the clean white sheets she had put on the bed for them, on the grounds that sheets were 'for dead folk'. For those who were prepared to get into bed, bedwetting was a common problem – again often put down to some sort of degeneracy among the evacuees, but in fact more to do with stress (large numbers of the British Expeditionary Force, returning from Dunkirk, suffered a similar problem).

> Colonel Blimp explains: 'Gad sir, Lord Mingy was right! To give the children of the unemployed enough to eat is to sap their sturdy British independence!'

More worryingly, an estimated 10 per cent of the child evacuees were unfamiliar with the workings of a flush toilet and thought that a newspaper in the corner of the room performed the same function. Equally difficult were the cases where evacuees from more comfortable inner city homes were exposed to the extremes of rural poverty.

Further tensions arose where the mothers of young children were evacuated. Two women sharing a kitchen often proved to be one too many, and rules (sometimes wholly Draconian and unreasonable rules) were set down for the terms of occupancy of the house. The following example of such house rules led to a prosecution:

> No access to the kitchen or bathroom; loan of crockery refused; no laundry to be carried out on the premises; charge of 1*s* per week for electric light; all residents to be home by 10.30 p.m.; residents to be out of the house between 10.00 a.m. and 8.30 p.m. on Sundays; no smoking; absolute quiet at all times; residents also had to leave the house whenever the proprietor went to visit her invalid mother [though they were allowed to await her return in the porch or in the summer house in the garden].

This hostess (if such she can be called) was fined £15 and 3 guineas costs.

Even where less extreme restrictions were applied, the evacuee mother and her child would in many cases find themselves without any normal domestic responsibilities or their usual circle of social contacts. They might find themselves out of the house for many hours of the day, killing time. Few areas initially had any recreational facilities for them, and their enforced idleness no doubt added to the evacuees' reputation for fecklessness. This can be seen in the following report of a county organiser

for the Women's Voluntary Service in one of the reception areas in
September 1939:

> I think this scheme is impracticable and unworkable, and it can never be
> successful. The low, slum type form the majority of the mothers, some of them out
> for what they can get, most of them dirty, many of them idle and unwilling to
> work or pull their weight. No arrangements whatever have been made for them by
> the local authorities from the social point of view. They have nowhere to go, and
> walk the streets tiring out themselves and their tiny children. . . .
>     The general feeling is that people can cope with the children and in time can
> get them clean and disciplined, but the mothers who are not a good influence are
> a great drawback. . . .
>     There is nowhere for them to go. That they are a bad slum type and expect 'the
> pub and the pictures' on the doorstep is not the point. Some arrangements should
> be made immediately for a mothers' club or recreation room for them. . . .
>     I feel that the dirt and low standard of living of the evacuees from big industrial
> cities of Leeds and Hull has been an eye-opener and an unpleasant shock to the
> inhabitants of an agricultural county like Lincolnshire, who had no idea that such
> terrible conditions existed.

The Women's Institute made its protests known through a report called
*Town Children through Country Eyes*, compiled from the experiences in some
1,700 of their branches of the appalling condition and habits of the
evacuee children. Copies were sent to Health and Education Officers of all
the towns and cities from which evacuees were sent.

One complaint the report may not have mentioned was that some of the
evacuated women – with their alleged fondness for a good time in all its
respects – also became rather too attractive to some of the more easily led
menfolk in the reception areas. In the eyes of some in the host areas,
evacuees also became synonymous with crime. Thus, one mother felt able
to plead in mitigation for her son, brought up before the court for the theft
of a mouth organ: 'He is a good boy at home. I think he has been
associating with evacuees.'

In Chester the local representative for the National Society for the
Prevention of Cruelty to Children tried to have an 8 p.m. curfew imposed
on the city's new guests. He was told that the magistrates had no such
powers, and that he should direct his idea to the Home Secretary.

---

A LIVERPOOL EVACUEE'S FIRST POSTCARD HOME

Dear Mum,

I hope you are well. I don't like the man's face much. Perhaps it will
look better in daylight. I like the dog's face best.

There were those who saw evacuation as an opportunity for social engineering on a large scale. This correspondent to *The Times*, for example, wanted to see the most disadvantaged children taken away from their parents entirely and placed into care:

> In the course of my work I have, in the last few years, attended many trials at the Central Criminal Court, and I am always nearly horrified by the low mental and physical standards of the accused persons. Stunted, misshapen creatures, only capable of understanding the very simplest language and quite incapable of thought, moved by impulses at the best sentimental, at the worst brutal. During a trial when the accused and witnesses are of this sub-human sort, it is as though a flat stone in the garden had been raised and pale, wriggling things, that had never seen the light had been exposed.
>
> These children, of whom the country residents so reasonably complain, are bound to grow up into just such sub-human savages, unless we seize this opportunity of saving them. . . . War has lifted the flat stone – these disgraces to our educational system have been forced out into the light. . . .

All manner of other problems were laid at the doors of the evacuees. It was said that their presence in local schools prejudiced the chances of local children getting scholarships for direct grant schools; that evacuation had disintegrated the life of the country and disrupted the trade of the urban areas, in both respects weakening the nation's war efforts; transport and communications had been disrupted, and (for reasons which are not immediately obvious) the government's market schemes for meat and fish had failed because of them; verminous evacuees had contaminated the wallpaper, furniture and bedding in their billets, leading to demands for compensation; helpless husbands, unable to look after themselves after their wives had been evacuated, were calling for more communal feeding; jury trials could not function in urban areas subject to substantial evacuation (the 1939 Administration of Criminal Justice Act actually made provision for trials to be held before juries of seven people – rather than twelve – at the Central Criminal Court); and local authorities were suffering loss of revenue.

Even insurance proved to be an unexpected complication. Early in 1940 the insurance companies announced that they would invoke a 'war clause' if householders made claims on their home or contents insurance resulting from the presence of evacuees. Despite exhortations from the British government, only one company – Lloyds – withdrew that clause. This proved to be a significant problem in at least one case. A church organisation, the Society for Waifs and Strays, bought two properties in Morthoe for the housing of evacuees. They were poorly supervised, and by the end of the war vandalism damage to them from the inmates was estimated at £1,500. A reluctant government found itself being badgered to honour claims such as these.

Objections to receiving evacuees took all forms. Didcot Parish Council pleaded exemption on the grounds that there were government stores and a railway junction (both potential bombing targets) nearby. A local authority in Wiltshire argued its case for not taking them in terms of the local shortage of domestic servants. For some, the dispute was more ideological. This letter to the *North Wales Chronicle* in January 1939 was from the Welsh Nationalist Party:

> The indiscriminate transfer of English people into Wales will place the Welsh language, and even the very existence of the Welsh nation, in jeopardy. The national welfare of the Welsh people should be a matter of first consideration by the authorities who are planning evacuation into the countryside. We, as Nationalists, demand that there should be no transfer of population into Wales which would endanger Welsh nationality. If England cannot make its emergency plans without imperilling the life of our little nation, let England renounce war and grant us self-government.

Small wonder that Hitler saw the nationalist parties as possible territory for Fifth Column activity. However, the Welsh Nationalists were not opposed to all evacuation. They protested against the decision of the Anderson Committee to designate south Wales as a 'neutral' area, and thus not to be evacuated, and called upon children from the valleys to be moved to safety (in rural Wales, naturally). They also wanted the children of Welsh expatriates in England to be evacuated to the land of their fathers, for a proper upbringing.

The Welsh antipathy to foreigners was reciprocated by some of their visitors. One Catholic priest from Liverpool called for children billeted in chapel-going Wales to be repatriated, since he felt that the physical danger they faced in Liverpool was far outweighed by the spiritual danger of exposure to such a heretical environment. Other Liverpool children found themselves thrown into Welsh village schools where both the religion and the language in which the lessons were taught were foreign. Some rose to the challenge, becoming fluent Welsh speakers and competing successfully in Eisteddfods.

Not everyone reacted with horror and resentment towards the evacuees, as this letter shows: 'I never knew that such conditions existed, and I feel ashamed of having been so ignorant of my neighbours. For the rest of my life I mean to try and make amends by helping such people to live cleaner and healthier lives.' The author could perhaps afford to take a more positive view, as he was not likely to be asked to take any evacuees himself. It was from Neville Chamberlain to his sister.

Supervision of the evacuated children became an increasing problem. Initially, around 103,000 inner city teachers and volunteer helpers were evacuated to look after the 827,000 primary school evacuees, a

A London Evacuee sees his First Cow

Much fun was made of the evacuees' ignorance of country matters. This item, quoted in Westall, appeared on the BBC News on 29 October 1939:

'The cow is a mamal [sic]. It has six sides, right, left, an upper and below. At the back is a tail, on which hangs a brush. With this, it sends the flies away so they do not fall in the milk. The head is for the purpose of growing horns and so that the mouth can be somewhere. The horns are to butt with and the mouth is to moo with. Under the cow hangs the milk. It is arranged for milking. When people milk, the milk comes and there is never an end to the supply. How the cow does it, I have not realised but it makes more and more. The cow has a fine sense of smell; one can smell it far away. This is the reason for the fresh air in the country.

'The man cow is called an ox. It is not a mamal. The cow does not eat much but what it eats, it eats twice so that it gets enough. When it is hungry it moos and when it says nothing it is because its inside is full up with grass.'

pupil:teacher ratio of 8:1. However, many of these volunteers proved to be unsuited to the job and 32,000 had been dismissed by the middle of 1941. Together with natural wastage among the teaching staff, this meant that the pupil:teacher ratio dropped to more like 100:1. Repeated government circulars urged host authorities to visit the home of each evacuee on at least a monthly basis, but this was often disregarded. Even where it was done, much could happen to the children between visits, and intimidation of the evacuees could prevent the authorities from finding out what was really going on.

There are many vivid accounts published of evacuees' experiences – good and bad. It would be impossible to say whether the good experiences outweigh the bad, but where they were bad, they could be very bad indeed. One former evacuee recalled, as a ten-year-old child, trying to cut her own throat with a knife (which fortunately turned out to be too blunt for the purpose). In another family of nine, the eldest five were sexually assaulted, an experience which meant that one of them was still receiving counselling forty years later. A man in Swanage was found guilty of indecently assaulting the three evacuees in his care, offering in his defence the improbable explanation that he was simply using them in bed as human hot water bottles.

EVACUEES' TALES

'I was soundly beaten at least once a week with sticks, poker, wooden spoon – whatever was at hand – mostly when the husband was at work. It was hard to endure this physical and mental abuse and I often thought of suicide by drowning myself in the fen drain a couple of hundred yards from the house. . . . I suffered from severe headaches and vomiting and trembled continuously with anxiety. I had outbreaks of sores on my scalp, face and body as well as hurting all over from the beatings. I was always hungry and had a bad case of intestinal worms of which only I was aware.'

John, aged about five, quoted by Wicks.

'Every item was stolen. All our toys, all our clothing that would fit members of other families, and they dictated our letters. . . . My sister Anne had beautiful long hair and it was falling out. And my hair started falling out. And scabs were coming on our heads and bodies.'

London boy, quoted by Grafton.

'It was there that I had my first experience with a man that was not quite nice. He would tuck me in of a night and fondle me. I was terrified. Mind you, he never forced me. He would just say that I was an evacuee and if I said anything he would send me back to where I'd be bombed. . . . Then one day I really got frightened. I thought he was going to put his thing inside me and I got really scared.'

Maureen, aged twelve, quoted by Wicks.

The failure of heavy bombing to materialise in the early months of the war led many evacuees to abandon their new living arrangements. The *Maidenhead Advertiser* reported in February 1940:

It is now known that, generally speaking, 59 per cent of the mothers and children moved to safety on the eve of the war have returned home. Locally, of course, the figure is more like 80 per cent, both in the Borough and the rural district, an appalling percentage. Something like half a million children evacuated to safe areas are still there, but about 43 per cent of the 734,883 school children evacuated have returned. . . . It is time to ask whether evacuation has been such a failure as to determine expert and general opinion that no such movement of children must be attempted again.

Evacuation was originally planned as a temporary and quasi-military operation to save children and mothers from a few weeks of intensive bombing. Whitehall did not foresee a complete and prolonged dislocation of normal education, and emergency education policy has been and is being built together in bits and pieces, generally following rather than leading public opinion and the education authorities. . . .

According to official figures, almost 900,000 evacuees had returned home by 8 January 1940. But the drift back to the cities brought new problems. The government had worked on the assumption that there would be total evacuation by the target groups. (Compulsory evacuation had been considered, but public opinion and the difficulty of enforcing it led the government to shy away from the idea.) Most of the inner-city schools had been closed, so those children who had stayed behind or had returned from evacuation were free to roam the streets all day and, if they were so inclined, get up to mischief. The Home Secretary was eventually forced to allow head teachers to reopen inner-city schools, always assuming they were not counted among the two-thirds of all inner-city schools taken over by ARP wardens or other parts of the war effort. Some, such as the Chief Education Officer for Sheffield, resorted to more radical solutions:

> I knew we had 55,000 children and no schools open . . . we appealed for 5,000 school rooms in private houses, for which we paid 2s 6d a week, and we moved the desks and furniture from the schools into those houses. The children were divided into groups of twelve and each group was taught for an hour and a half a day . . . they spent another hour and a half in the local library.

Instead, the government tried to force evacuation by the back door, by means of making life as unpleasant as possible for those who remained in the cities. In London it became illegal to take your children into the tube shelters during the 'epidemic period' from 15 January to 31 March. No clue was given as to what the expected epidemic was and none was subsequently reported. This was coupled with increased enforcement of legislation relating to child abuse, school attendance and measures against those living in unsanitary conditions. Life in the tube shelters was also more closely regulated. You needed a ticket from the authorities to occupy a place in them and you could be ejected from them, if the authorities saw fit.

## THE POOR HOUSING THE POOR

> We find over and over again that it is the really poor people who are willing to take evacuees and that the sort of bridge-playing set who live in such places as Chorley Wood are terribly difficult about it all.
>
> WVS Regional Administrator

While the evacuation programme gave some of its participants a terrifying view across the gulf that divided the classes, for the most part the official scheme involved the poor housing the poor. Some owners of large country homes threw open their doors generously to the newcomers, but Home Intelligence reports in June 1941 showed that billeting officers were generally afraid to press the owners of large country houses to take evacuees, for fear of reprisals. They would have to live in that community after the war. The use of local agents as billeting officers was generally felt to be 'a bad idea' for this reason, and local or central government officers were suggested instead. One billeting officer even tried to discourage one big house owner from taking evacuees, for fear that he would be 'letting down' the owners of other big houses locally, who were holding out against it. More generally, the fact that only a quarter of the original offers of billeting were taken up, owing to the lower than expected numbers of evacuees, meant that the burden was falling unevenly on a small proportion of households. A campaign was run to move the evacuees about, to share the burden more equally.

## THE END OF EVACUATION

The scheme was a long time ending – at least officially. Delayed by the V1 and V2 flying bombs, it was April 1945 before the government issued Circular 68/45, which set out the arrangements for bringing the evacuees home. However, many of them had not waited for the government's permission – in the six months to March 1945, it was estimated that 600,000 out of the 1.04 million remaining evacuees had repatriated themselves. For many of the rest, things were far less straightforward. Many were returning to areas which had suffered widespread devastation from the bombers, and pre-war housing problems were exacerbated by the chronic post-war shortage of housing in the urban areas. By August 1945 there were still 76,000 evacuees with no homes to return to.

Some children – an estimated 5,200 – were still left unaccounted for when the scheme was ended in March 1946. Many were believed to have been orphaned by the blitz. Others, who for example had changed billets without informing the authorities, were effectively 'mislaid'.

But even those who could return often found it hard to readjust. For the evacuees, some were traumatised by their experiences of poverty or child abuse; conversely, for those who had passed the war years in a more comfortable billet, the return to urban deprivation could be an equal shock. Children who had grown used to the countryside found it hard to re-adapt to a harsher urban environment; some parents found it difficult to adjust to the loss of a child-free independence. For others, the bond between child and parent had been broken entirely; they met at the railway station as strangers, and some even failed to recognise each other at all. For those returning from evacuation overseas, the drabness of austerity Britain was sometimes the hardest thing to bear.

## THE PROBLEMS WITH EVACUATION

At least some of the problems resulting from evacuation can be laid at the door of appeasement. Chamberlain and his Cabinet were desperate not to be seen to be putting Britain on to a war footing, lest it undermined their efforts to negotiate peace terms. This was one of the main reasons why the preparations were made in secret; as a result, key players were not consulted and did not tie their parts of the programme together. It also put the evacuation scheme in direct conflict with other government programmes, for example where the demands of evacuation were made on communities whose housing supply was already being stretched by the demands of billeted service personnel.

The other reason for secrecy was concern that the very sight of the preparations would cause widespread panic among the people. During the Munich crisis, there had been panic buying and a flight from the cities, with 150,000 people heading for the hills of Wales. Earlier planning for air raids had even toyed with the idea of throwing a giant police and army cordon around London, to prevent a mass evacuation. However, in the end, secrecy about war preparations could hardly be consistent with digging a million feet of slit trenches in the capital's parks and issuing the entire population with gas-masks.

A degree of panic also entered into the execution of the scheme, in particular because it was done before there was any firm indication of the German intention to commence bombing. This stems back to the wildly exaggerated estimates of the effects of bombing, discussed earlier. At least some of the resentment of the hosts might have been eased, had they been able to see a good reason for the cities being evacuated.

The planning of the evacuation also concentrated on the arrangements in the evacuation areas, rather than on those at the reception end. This was perhaps inevitable, given the much more diffuse nature of the reception areas and the limited resources of many of the rural district councils who were charged with making the arrangements. At this time, the ability of any authority, in particular the smaller rural ones, to deliver social services was very limited by modern standards. This was still the era of the Victorian Poor Laws – in 1939 a hundred thousand people were still cared for in workhouses. Such arrangements as the receiving authorities did make were not helped by the fact that the numbers and types of evacuees delivered to them often differed wildly from what they had been led to expect.

Nor had the (presumably) middle-class people who organised the arrangements had the slightest inkling of the shock waves this enforced breaking down of the class barriers would create. Their initial assumption, that working-class mothers would be as willing as their middle-class counterparts to part with their young children, proved wrong, leading to the piecemeal nature of the evacuation and the problems associated with that. And if any of them entertained fond notions that it would lead to a breaking down of class barriers, this was soon dispelled by the wave of recrimination among the hosts against what they saw as feckless and work-shy parents, who let their children leave home in such a state of health, hygiene and dress.

## EVACUATION AND THE RICH

Those who could afford it made their own evacuation plans. In addition to the official evacuation scheme, an estimated two million people made such arrangements. Some were able to stay with family or friends in less dangerous parts of the country, while those who had the money bought or rented somewhere safe. Out-of-the-way hotels advertised their services to 'the sensitive and artistic' who wished to be well out of the conflict. These became derisively known as 'funk holes', and the *Daily Express* journalist Nathaniel Gubbins created the fictional population of the 'Safe Hotel'. *The Times* said: 'The hotels are filled with well-to-do refugees, who too often have fled from nothing. They sit and read and knit and eat and drink, and get no nearer the war than the news they read in the newspapers.'

> Colonel Blimp explains: 'Gad sir, Lucy Houston is right! We need 5,000 more planes, otherwise how can the upper classes fly to Scotland when the bombing of London begins?'

Private evacuees also took up a good deal of the accommodation that might otherwise have been available for the government scheme. Potential hosts often decided that they represented a 'nicer class of person' than the urban poor that might be visited upon them under the official scheme. A 1939 survey showed that 18 per cent of all the billeting accommodation in England and Wales had been pre-booked seven months before the war broke out. In desirable areas like West Sussex, Berkshire and Herefordshire, the figure was over 25 per cent. Constantine Fitzgibbon recalls:

. . . a constant stream of private cars and London taxis driving up to mother's front door in the Thames Valley in the September of 1939, filled with men and women of all ages, in various stages of hunger, exhaustion and fear, offering absurd sums for accommodation in her already overcrowded house and even for

---

PET EVACUEES

In some cases, pets were treated better than human evacuees. Many people were killing their pets as war broke out and evacuation started. Prompted by this, the Animal Defence League started a scheme for evacuating dogs. The Duchess of Hamilton threw open the grounds of her Dorset estate to them and 176 dogs were eventually resident there. The staff even wrote to the owners at intervals, informing them of the progress of their pets. But for those pets who could not get away from it all, there was always: 'Bob Martins Fit and Hysteria Powders in ARP cartons to calm cats and dogs in air raids.'

---

food. This horde of satin-clad, pinstriped refugees poured through for two or three days, eating everything that was for sale, downing all the spirits in the pubs, and then vanished.

## OVERSEAS EVACUATION

Safer still were non-combatant countries. It was reported that, in the forty-eight hours leading up to the start of the official evacuation, some five thousand people had embarked at Southampton for the United States, and places on board any remaining ships were at a premium.

Offers to give a home to a British evacuee child came from all over the Americas and the Commonwealth. American corporations offered to take the children of their UK employees; American doctors offered to take the children of their professional counterparts in Britain; Rhodes scholars were encouraged to offer places to the children of Oxbridge and other dons; Douglas Fairbanks Junior proposed setting up a colony of British actors' children in Hollywood. The elite Cambridge Tutoring School in New York offered to take a hundred British boys at the bargain price of £100 each, but specified that: 'Boys from a cultural background only can be accepted. Sons of army and navy officers and professionals would be welcome.' They even offered to send the private yacht of one of their patrons to collect the boys, but this elitist offer was not taken up. While the Commonwealth countries were generally happy to receive a cross-section of British youth, the Americans were more likely to want children from 'a better background'.

There was criticism, from Labour MPs and others, of the elitist nature of private evacuation arrangements, the cost of which placed them far beyond the means of the ordinary citizen. Initially, offers from overseas governments to take British children through some official scheme were dismissed by the government as 'good hearted but impracticable'. The idea was ruled out for fear that it would result in panic and defeatism, and lead to resentment among those left behind. There were also practical problems, such as the shortage of space on ships to transport them, the lack of military vessels to provide an escort, and the resultant danger of the exercise.

None the less a parliamentary committee was set up to examine the question in more detail, under Geoffrey Shakespeare MP. It reported to the War Cabinet on 17 June 1940, and it was while they were actually making their presentation that news was brought in to the Cabinet Room of France's surrender. Churchill was said – perhaps not surprisingly – to have been so preoccupied with the news of the surrender that he failed to notice that a decision had been made about the evacuation matter.

The result was that an organisation – the Children's Overseas Reception Board (CORB) – was set up, to coordinate the evacuation of children, principally to America. The scheme was drawn up with a strongly egalitarian emphasis, with at least 90 per cent of the intake coming from state schools, and particular priority being given to children from poorer backgrounds and the most vulnerable areas. News of this scheme was made public on 19 June, and by mid-morning a queue 3,000 strong had formed outside the CORB offices. They were forced hurriedly to issue a statement to try to calm the rush – emphasising the dangers involved and the limited numbers of spaces available.

It had little effect. By 4 July they had received a total of 211,548 applications, almost 200,000 of them from state-aided schools and almost 50 per cent of the applications meeting the eligibility criteria. On that day, the government closed the waiting list and temporarily suspended the scheme, because of the lack of Royal Navy escorts for the convoys concerned. Private evacuations meanwhile continued unabated, and there were further complaints in Parliament that the CORB scheme had just been a ruse to allow the government to get the children of the well-to-do out of the country without undue criticism.

There were further delays later that month, and it was 21 July before the first of CORB's evacuees could sail. They were taken to Liverpool, where they were housed in children's homes and schools, pending their departure. (Private evacuees leaving from Liverpool at the same time were, by contrast, put up at the Adelphi Hotel.) It did not take long for the dangers involved in the enterprise to become clear. On 1 August the ship *Volendam*, with 321 evacuees among its 606 passengers, was torpedoed. Fortunately, the damage was not terminal and the ship was towed back to port by tugs. However, it transpired that *Volendam* had been sailing in a vulnerable position at the head of one of the lines of the convoy, and she was also carrying a cargo of wheat that made her a legitimate target for the U-boats.

## BUT WORSE WAS TO COME

On Friday 13 September 1940 the Glasgow-built ship *City of Benares* pulled out of Liverpool, bound for Canada. It was an inauspicious date for such a hazardous journey. Three hundred passengers were on board, including a large group of child evacuees. Six hundred miles out, at ten o'clock on a moonlit night, the ship was struck by a torpedo on the port side, immediately below the children's quarters. One child was killed outright and many more were injured. Attempts were made to lower the boats, but eleven of the twelve took in water as they hit the rough sea. One, containing the captain, sank completely. Most of the children remained calm, but the largely Indian crew panicked. They were among the first into the boats and, once there, most took no further part in the rescue. The nearest civilian ship to them, the SS *Marina*, was also torpedoed, and the nearest Royal Navy ship, the destroyer *Hurricane*, was sixteen hours away – despite the fact that the *City of Benares* was supposed to be escorted.

Almost immediately, bad weather set in. Rain and hail added to the waves that were sweeping over the boats faster than the survivors could bail. They found themselves up to their knees or even their chests in water. It became dangerous to move in the boats, since a foot in the wrong place could mean capsize and people being swept overboard.

In one of the boats Michael Rennie, a 23-year-old theology student, found himself in charge of fourteen children and two adults. In the days that followed, he repeatedly dived overboard to rescue one or other of his party who had been swept out of the boat. It was after fourteen days in the lifeboat that they saw the Royal Navy coming. Rennie leapt to his feet, waving and shouting 'Hurrah! Here comes the destroyer, thank God!' They were his last words. Fatally weakened by his ordeal, he lost his balance and fell overboard. Efforts by the others in the lifeboat to save him were futile. The government turned a deaf ear to calls for him to be awarded a posthumous George Cross, and his parents were even made to repay the loan he had taken out to get him through university.

A happier fate awaited the Catholic priest Father O'Sullivan, who was in bed with chronic seasickness when the torpedo struck. He rounded up his party of children and they were rescued after eight days in the lifeboat. Back in England, he found that he had been declared dead, and had the grim satisfaction of reading his own glowing obituaries.

There were 84 children among the 260 people who died on the *City of Benares*, and world opinion was outraged. The Germans first tried to deny the event entirely, then accused the British of using the children as a shield to try to secure safe passage for legitimate military targets. This disaster effectively marked the end of the government-sponsored overseas evacuation scheme.

The government had not at any stage been happy about the scheme. As Winston Churchill put it:

> I must frankly admit that the full bearings of this question were not appreciated by the British Government at the time it was first raised. It was not foreseen that the mild countenance given to this plan would lead to a movement of such dimensions and that a crop of alarmist and depressing rumours would follow at its tail, detrimental to the interest of national defence.

At home, the scheme was regarded as pushing the panic button. Abroad, the Germans made propaganda out of it, and used the Americans' increasing involvement to cast doubts on their neutrality. However, private evacuations continued after this time, until late 1941. It is thought that some 17,000 private evacuees were sent abroad after June 1940. The elitist nature of this trade was by now very clear; social gadfly Henry 'Chips' Channon recalled in his diary for June 1940 visiting Euston station, dispatching his offspring on the train to Liverpool Docks: 'There was a queue of Rolls-Royces and liveried servants and mountains of trunks. It seemed that everyone we knew was there.'

The list of evacuees did indeed read like a version of *Who's Who*. As well as Channon's son (Paul Channon, later himself a Conservative cabinet minister), there were the wife and children of Lord Mountbatten, the son of the Minister of Information, Duff Cooper, and members of the Guinness, Rothschild and Hambro families. Also among those evacuated were future politicians Jeremy Thorpe and Shirley Williams. At least three sitting MPs fled the country. This export industry became a sufficient embarrassment for the British government to lead the Home Secretary, Sir John Anderson, to suggest scrapping the exit permit scheme, to avoid accusations of elitism. However, the Cabinet rejected this as 'unduly drastic'.

The warmth of the welcomes for British children began to cool more than somewhat as the war went on. The Americans had their first taste of rationing after Pearl Harbor, further dampening their enthusiasm for their guests. By 1944, Lord Halifax, who had by then become British Ambassador to the United States, reported that 'nearly every evacuee family is . . . producing a festering spot of anti-British feeling'.

Their hosts had not expected them to stay for more than a year, but once the threat of invasion receded, the British government seemed strangely reluctant to take its citizens back. One of the reasons given for this was the danger involved in shipping them back, though this was greatly reduced compared with the risks faced on the outward journey.

Wealthy people evacuating their children to the Dominions when invasion threatened in 1940 increased class animosity at the time. Home Intelligence reported on this in July 1940, when the CORB scheme had originally been postponed:

There is great disappointment at the postponement of the plan for evacuating children to the Dominions. There was initial resistance among the public to sending children abroad: vigorous publicity overcame that resistance, and the results of a statistical survey showed that the parents of approximately 1,000,000 children were prepared for them to go. The effect of a reversal of policy has promoted sharp recrimination against the rich, whose children were enabled to sail.

Now, as parents waited anxiously for the return of their children, there was a further public outcry against the 'White Ensign' scheme, whereby the children of the rich and influential could get a preferential passage home on a Royal Navy ship. The government tried to play down the adverse publicity, claiming rather implausibly that they had no control over decisions made by individual captains. Thomas Cook also operated a scheme for shipping children back, for those for whom money was no object. Even the most nightmarish passages across the Atlantic, where the passengers faced everything from wet bedding and inedible food, through to sexual harassment and the theft of their luggage by the crew, commanded a hefty premium. Some American hosts were so keen to be rid of their young guests that they paid the fare for their parents!

But many could not afford to pay, and had no sponsor. By the end of 1943 there were almost twelve thousand women and children waiting to get back from the USA and Canada. Some waited over two years for a passage. The British government insisted on negotiating a safe conduct permit from the Germans before launching an official repatriation programme – something they had tried and failed to negotiate in the much more dangerous conditions of 1940. This further fuelled the speculation that, in the original evacuation, the British government had gambled with the children's lives against the possibility of drawing America into the war.

# THREE

# CLASS WAR

## THE WAR OF POLITICS

> Socialism is, in its essence, an attack not only on British enterprise but
> on the right of an ordinary man or woman to breathe freely without
> having a harsh, clumsy, tyrannical hand clapped across their mouth
> and nostrils.
>
> *Winston Churchill, election broadcast, 4 June 1945.*

The gulf between the classes manifested itself in many ways other than the
evacuation scheme. Britain entered the war a deeply divided society. The
depression of the 1930s had seen hunger marches and other
demonstrations on the streets of London. Attempts by the government to
address unemployment and poverty through measures such as the Land
Settlement Association – military-style camps to train the unemployed for a
career in an agricultural industry that was itself in deep recession – had
ended in a shambles, with accusations of them being 'slave camps'. Rent
strikes in the East End of London ended in battles between the tenants and
the police. The most basic social services were either severely means-tested
or available only through charity or the Victorian institutions of the Poor
Law.

   The idea that party political differences were shelved for the duration of
the war is some way from the truth. Entrenched political divisions were
maintained throughout the conflict, at times threatening the wartime
coalition and, at one point, actually bringing down the Conservative
government that had led the nation into war. Part of the problem lay in the
personalities of the wartime prime ministers. Taking Neville Chamberlain
first, there can rarely have been a prime minister less capable of uniting the
parliamentary parties against a common enemy. Chamberlain had utter
contempt for socialism and took little trouble to hide it. As Attlee put it: 'He
always treated us like dirt.' Even his own side acknowledged his
shortcomings in this respect. His Chief Whip, David Margesson: 'He
engendered personal dislike among his opponents to an extent almost
unbelievable. . . . I believe the reason was that his cold intellect was too
much for them, he beat them up in argument and debunked their
catchphrases.'

Some on the Labour side before the war were almost more inclined to blame Chamberlain than Hitler for the forthcoming hostilities. Ernest Bevin, then leader of the Transport and General Workers' Union, put it thus to the 1939 Labour Party Conference:

> Behind Chamberlain are the bankers; they are the principal supporters of appeasement for Germany. They do not want justice for the German masses – that is quite a different thing. I am anxious to prevent this movement fighting for the preservation of the Paris Bourse, the London Stock Exchange, the Amsterdam Exchange and Wall Street.

Similar views were picked up by Home Intelligence from working-class respondents, reflecting on the possibility of Hitler invading: 'He won't hurt us; it's the bosses he's after; we'll probably be better off when he comes; he robs the rich to pay the poor; German victory would only harm the wealthy.'

The government even considered plans for a campaign to highlight the sufferings of the rich in wartime, but wisely abandoned the idea. The Ministry of Information's Home Morale Emergency Committee none the less saw class feeling as a major factor undermining war morale and proposed that:

> . . . something might be done to diminish the present predominance of the cultured voice upon the wireless. Every effort should be made to bring working-class people to the microphone and more frequent use should be made of left-wing speakers to counteract the propaganda of our enemies regarding imperialism and capitalism.

The labour movement had bitter memories of war and its aftermath. After the sacrifices made by millions of the working classes on the fields of France and elsewhere in 1914–18, they saw war profiteers make huge fortunes while their people were forced into unemployment and poverty by the post-war depression. Chamberlain proposed some modest preparations for war – controls over wages, strikes and labour supply – during the early part of 1939. Even he realised that he needed cooperation from the labour movement for these preparations, and that this would not be forthcoming without some controls over profiteering. Chamberlain therefore promised 'to take the profit out of war', by introducing an excess wartime profits tax. This came in, at a rate of 60 per cent, at the outbreak of war. But when he set up a Ministry of Supply in July 1939 to implement some of these proposals, its advisory panel was drawn solely from the management side of industry – no trade union representatives were invited to take part.

The class war thus continued scarcely unabated into the early 'phoney war' period of the conflict. Certain concessions were made by the

Conservative government to reduce the normal acrimony of party dispute – shadow ministers were taken to some extent into the confidence of their opposite numbers in government – but Chamberlain's whole pursuit of the war was based upon the premise that it would all blow over without too much serious fighting. His view was that Hitler would not dare to expose his people to the potential suffering of a second major conflict in twenty years. He therefore attempted to conduct the war with a minimum of disruption to 'business as usual'. This meant giving as few concessions as possible to the opposition, so that there was less to unpick later. It certainly excluded setting up the kind of coalition government established by Lloyd George in 1916 (in which one of the most conspicuous failures had been the Co-ordinator for National Service – one Neville Chamberlain).

Gradually, pressure grew for greater control of the economy and for more vigorous efforts to put it on a war footing. Under Chamberlain, the whole management of the economy seemed positively amateurish. Even the government's Chief Economic Adviser, Lord Stamp, was only a part-time appointment. The half of the week he did not devote to steering the nation's economy was given over to running the London and North Eastern Railway.

Even the early proposals to put Britain on a war footing ran into difficulty, so deep was the class divide. The economist Keynes proposed introducing compulsory saving, to take some of the spending power of the working class out of the economy in order to fund the war effort. Even though this was to be offset by minimum standards of living for the lower-paid, Ernest Bevin opposed it. He anticipated the workers being asked to fund the prosecution of the war and then being faced with bearing the burden of unemployment afterwards. At the same time the Conservatives instinctively recoiled from greater state planning of the war economy. So, in the early part of 1940, little progress was made in preparing for a war that seemed an awfully long time coming.

> Colonel Blimp explains:
> 'To preserve British liberty, we must lock up the entire British Labour Party.'

Meanwhile the tensions in Parliament were starting to re-emerge. The main parties had entered into a pact to ensure that by-elections would not be contested, leaving the sitting party to replace vacancies. By the spring of 1940 Labour's dislike of the Chamberlain government was such that the party conference had no fewer than fifty-one resolutions on the agenda to abandon the by-election truce.

When Chamberlain was displaced as prime minister, it was not the votes of his own party that finally unseated him. For two days after the confidence vote, Chamberlain still entertained hopes of leading a coalition of some description. It was Attlee's telephone call, saying that Labour would not serve in a Chamberlain-led government, that forced his resignation. By this time, the pressure for coalition was irresistible and Labour, although heavily outnumbered in Parliament, were able at last to extract their revenge on a hated prime minister.

That is not to say that Labour's relations with Churchill were anywhere near idyllic. His track record was, from a Labour perspective, perfectly appalling. During his previous time as Home Secretary, in 1910, he was credited in Labour mythology (wrongly, as it happens) with having instructed troops to fire on striking miners at Tonypandy. He had also been bitterly opposed to the General Strike of 1926, editing the strike-breaking newspaper, the *British Gazette*. On foreign policy, Churchill had advocated the use of force to put down the Russian Revolution, had ridiculed Gandhi and praised both Mussolini and Franco. The ideological gulf between him and Labour was to remain vast throughout the war.

Churchill was not even particularly secure among his own party, prior to rejoining the Cabinet. His own constituency party had agreed to continue supporting him in 1938–9 by only a single vote, and his active support within the parliamentary party was limited to a tiny group. However, as war approached and his stand against appeasement was vindicated, he began to rehabilitate himself in public opinion. By May 1939, 56 per cent of the population wanted him back in the Cabinet (though a significant 26 per cent did not). Even then, he was not an obvious choice for prime minister. In April 1940, 57 per cent of the public were still in favour of Chamberlain remaining as prime minister, and on his departure the following month, the majority of the party establishment (and the royal family) favoured Lord Halifax as his successor. It was only the fact that Halifax did not want the job that created the opening for Churchill.

Chamberlain may have thought that the war could be conducted as an extension of normal business but, even among those who accepted the need for a more radical approach, party interests were not abandoned for the duration. Each side always had at the back of its mind the resumption of normal party politics at the end of hostilities. As Churchill put it to a meeting of senior Conservatives in March 1942, when the war was over, he wanted the Conservatives to be seen as 'the main part of the rock on which the salvation of Britain was founded and the freedom of mankind regained'.

Clearer thinkers among the Conservatives foresaw the sea change that the war would bring to the political scene. Robert Boothby wrote to Lloyd George in the following terms, expressing views that were also, to varying degrees, being articulated by others, such as Eden and Butler:

> Nothing is more certain than that this war will mark the transition from monopoly capitalism to socialism. . . . You cannot hope to go through a world convulsion of this magnitude without fundamental changes in the social as well as the economic structure. It is inconceivable to me that our present hereditary system, or our 'caste' system of education, can survive the struggle without drastic modification. In the case of Churchill, any diminution of the power of the governing class will involve a clash between his natural instincts and his imagination.

Labour moved quickly to articulate its aims, both for the war and for the peace that would follow. They published their document, *Labour's Aims in War and Peace*, during the period of the phoney war. The *Birmingham Mail*, speaking from Chamberlain's heartland, was predictably scathing about its programme of nationalisation, increased public works and improved social services:

> Where . . . will the money come from? The answer, alas, is far from reassuring at the moment. For the raising of revenue for the prosecution of its vigorous social policy, the Labour Party proposes to revise dramatically the system of death duties, to steepen the graduation of income tax and to tax excess profit and 'all other forms of wealth'. With the best will in the world for the England that is to be, our own optimism wavers a little at this point.

Churchill and the Conservatives had, to a far greater degree, to be persuaded that the aim of the war was something more than just beating Hitler. They kept much more silent about the world after the war and, when peace arrived, tried to cry 'foul'. An exhibition entitled 'How the people were told a story' claimed in 1947 that socialist propaganda was promoted during the war years despite an alleged truce between the parties.

In these political terms, the conduct of the war can be seen as a long preparation for the election of 1945. One of the reasons for Labour's outstanding electoral success in that year was that they were associated in the public's mind with the successes of the war and with the reforms that were to follow it, while the Conservatives were seen as the 'old guard', still associated with the discredited policy of appeasement, and with many of the problems of the war years.

## CLASS WAR IN THE WORK PLACE

This was seen as the first real 'total war', in the sense that virtually every other aspect of life was subjugated to the war effort. It was a war that would be won as much in the factories as on the battlefields. But Britain in the 1930s had been riven with deep class divisions that were thrown into sharp relief by the recession. Far from the war effort sweeping away these

MARY NORDEN

# Decorative Embroidery

PHOTOGRAPHY BY SANDRA LANE

conran
OCTOPUS

**This book is dedicated to Sylvie,
with my love**

First published in 1997 by Conran Octopus Limited,
37 Shelton Street, London WC2H 9HN

*Commissioning editor* **Suzannah Gough**
*Project editor* **Helen Ridge**
*Assistant editor* **Tessa Clayton**
*Copy editor* **Alison Bolus**

*Art editor* **Alison Barclay**

*Illustrator* **Carolyn Jenkins**
*Stylist* **Mary Norden**

*Production* **Mano Mylvaganam**

A catalogue record for this book is
available from the British Library

ISBN 1 85029 856 4

PRINTED IN HONG KONG

# Contents

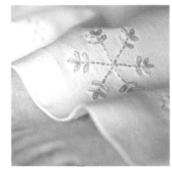
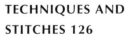

*I love the way a few simple stitches can transform an uninteresting piece of household linen or the plainest of fabrics into something special and unique – a white pillowcase embroidered with a monogram becomes exclusive, while a blue linen curtain needs no more than a border of simple posies to look exquisite.*

*Embroidery encompasses many different types of fabric decoration, some so beautiful and detailed that it is difficult to believe that a needle and thread created them. However, it is my aim to show that a design using one or two embroidery stitches can be just as effective, if not more so, as an ambitious piece worked in many stitches. For this book I have limited myself to fifteen elementary stitches and used them in a range of different, but straightforward, projects. Like any craft, embroidery is best learned by starting with the basics – jump too quickly into the deep end and you will almost certainly become disillusioned. But once you have mastered a few easy stitches and embroidered a design successfully, you will have the confidence to tackle more ambitious projects and may even feel inspired to create your own patterns.*

Mary Norden

Posies and Sprigs

FOR THE EMBROIDERER, flowers offer an endless source of inspiration. They can be translated into the simplest of garlands or into larger, more intricate bouquets. They can be used singly to embellish the centre of a cushion or the corner of a handkerchief, in rows to form exquisite decorative borders for sheets and curtains, or placed at random, reminiscent of simple eighteenth-century sprigged fabrics.

For a more traditional floral pattern, the shape and detail of each flower head will often dictate which stitches to use. The Sprays of Wild Flowers design is a good example of this. French knots make perfect flower stamens, while lazy daisy stitches are ideal for the long thin petals of daisies and cornflowers. For more abstract flowers and leaves, there is much more scope for experimenting with different stitches. The eight-petalled Stylized Blooms, embroidered in four different ways, could be worked with almost any combination of stitches, while the Delicate Posies design looks equally good stitched solidly in satin stitch or with each petal outlined in lazy daisy stitch.

The bold and interesting shapes of leaves also translate extremely well into embroidery. They are at their freshest when outlined with a simple stitch and worked in just one colour.

*LEFT: Just two simple stitches, stem and fern, convey beautifully the essence of a horse chestnut leaf. OPPOSITE: Simple bags made from remnants of raw silk and linen fabric are embroidered with bold stylized flowers in a mix of creamy colours.*

# DELICATE POSIES

ABOVE: The flower petals on this chair-back cover needed to be robust to withstand wear and tear, and were embroidered in padded satin stitch.
OPPOSITE: The petals on this curtain border were embroidered in delicate lazy daisy stitch.

Posies, like bouquets, have been a constant theme in fabric design, from the smallest, daintiest bunches to larger arrangements that combine a variety of flowers. Refreshingly simple and unpretentious, they are evocative of romance, gift-giving and the sentiments of spring and summer.

For the posy shown here, embroidered singly on the chair-back covers and repeated to form a border on the curtain, I used a simple palette of colours that gives the design a fresh appeal. In addition to variations in the scale and positioning of the posies, different effects are easy to achieve by varying the embroidery stitches.

## MATERIALS
- DMC stranded embroidery cotton in the following colours:
    cream 712
    pink 3687
    yellow 3822
    green 3347 (*curtain only*)
    Quantities for the curtain depend on the length of the border to be worked. One skein of cream is sufficient to embroider three complete posies. One skein of each of the other three colours will embroider as many as six posies.
    Cream was used for all three chair-back covers. For the green and yellow covers I worked the centre of the flowers in pink; for the pink cover I substituted yellow. For one posy enlarged to 20cm (8in) high I used two skeins of cream and half a skein at most of pink or yellow.

*For the curtain*
- plain blue linen fabric sufficient to make up one or two curtains to the required size

*For the chair-back cover(s)*
- 50 x 90cm (20 x 36in) of coloured cotton or linen fabric for each cover, or ready-made chair-back covers to fit your chairs
- 38 x 43cm (15 x 17in) thin foam pad(s), or correct size required to fit ready-made chair-back covers
- 40cm (16in) of 2.5cm (1in) wide cream cotton tape for each cover

*For all projects*
- tracing paper
- crewel (embroidery) needle size 6
- dressmaker's carbon paper
- embroidery hoop

## STITCHES USED
    French knot
    stem stitch
    lazy daisy stitch (*curtain only*)
    straight stitch (*curtain only*)
    padded satin stitch (*chair-back cover only*)
For full details on stitches, see pages 132–7.

## TECHNIQUES
For full practical information on methods used in this project, refer to Techniques on pages 129–31.

you will need 10cm (4in) for the heading and 10–20cm (4–8in) for the hem, depending on how deep you want it to be.

All the flower heads are worked with three strands of thread and the stems are worked with six strands. Start by stitching the flower heads, using cream thread and working each petal in lazy daisy stitch. With pink thread, work one small straight stitch at the top of each petal to cover the securing stitch (see illustration below). In the centre of each flower head work three or four French knots in yellow. Finally, work the green stems in stem stitch.

If you are embroidering a pair of curtains, reverse the pattern on the second curtain so that both sets of posies lean towards each other. To do this, turn the template over to give a mirror image. The template is suitable for a right-hand curtain; the photograph opposite shows the design on a left-hand curtain.

*RIGHT: After working each petal in lazy daisy stitch, colour each petal tip with one small straight stitch in pink. Bring the needle through to the right side at the tip of the petal and insert it inside so the coloured thread covers the stitch holding down the loop of the lazy daisy stitch.*

## To work the curtain

Trace the template above using the tracing paper or, if you require a larger posy, enlarge the template to the required size on a photocopier. Using a tape measure and sewing pins, plan the placement of the posies along the edge of the curtain fabric. I positioned each of my posy motifs 9cm (3½in) apart (measuring from the top of one motif to the bottom of the stems of the next), and 5cm (2in) from the outer edge. This latter measurement included a 2.5cm (1in) side hem allowance for making up the curtains. For a denser border pattern, position the flowers closer together. Use dressmaker's carbon paper to transfer the pattern. Do not extend the border too near the bottom or the top of the curtain;

## COLOUR GUIDE

Cream
712

Pink
3687

Yellow
3822

Green
3347

**To make up the curtain**

Make up the curtain(s) as required (depending on your choice of heading), using the hem and heading allowances. It is a good idea to line the curtain to protect the back of the embroidery.

**To work the chair-back cover**

If you are making your own cover, mark out two pieces of fabric, each measuring 38 x 43cm (15 x 17in). Add a 2cm (¾in) seam allowance all around, then cut out. Put one piece aside for backing.

Enlarge the posy template on page 14 to 180% on a photocopier. Using dressmaker's carbon paper, transfer the pattern onto the fabric. The best way to get the correct position is to fold the cover lengthways over the chair it is intended for. Alternatively, fold the fabric in half, then position the posy carefully in the centre of one half.

The flower petals are worked using three strands of thread and the flower centres and stems with six strands. Start by stitching the petals in padded satin stitch (referring to the template for the direction in which the stitches should run). In the centre of each flower work several French knots in pink or yellow to form a neat clump. For each stem work two rows of stem stitch in cream, narrowing to one row at the top to give a tapered effect.

## To make up the chair-back cover

Cut the tape into four equal parts. Position the pieces on top of the right side of the backing fabric, two on either side, 6cm (2½in) from the top and bottom edges (this includes the seam allowance). The tapes should be facing inwards. Sew securely 2cm (¾in) from the side edges. Place the embroidered piece and the backing fabric right sides together (making sure the tapes are inside) and pin. Sew together with a 2cm (¾in) seam, leaving a large enough opening for the foam pad to be inserted. Turn to the right side and press before inserting the pad. Close the opening with back or running stitch. Tie the tapes into bows.

*Three beautifully embroidered chair-back covers set the mood for a leisurely summer meal. If you prefer to use fabric in just one shade, vary the colour of each posy.*

# GARLANDS OF FLOWERS

*RIGHT: Decorate buttons with stylized flower heads, either embroidering the petals solidly with satin stitch, or delicately outlining the shape. OPPOSITE: Bed linen with embroidered floral borders makes a pretty impact.*

*A simple pattern of pink flowers linked by delicate curving stems gives starched sheets and pillowcases a romantic touch. This set of bed linen illustrates how four different border patterns can be achieved from just one design, either by varying the type of stitch used, or working only part of the template. The design would work equally well as a border for curtains or a tablecloth, or singly on buttons, as well as in numerous different colourways, from the palest of pastels to darker shades of blue.*

## MATERIALS

- DMC stranded embroidery cotton in the following colours:
  - pink 3607
  - red 606
  - green 704

  To embroider the single sheet, one skein of each colour is sufficient. For a double or king-size sheet, you will need a second skein of green and pink.
- plain cotton or linen sheet and pillowcases or, if you prefer to make your own, cotton sheeting
- small remnants of fine cotton or linen for buttons
- button-covering kits – these vary in size from 11–38mm (½–1½in) in diameter. I used sizes 22mm and 29mm (⅞in and 1³⁄₁₆in).
- tracing paper
- crewel (embroidery) needle size 6
- dressmaker's carbon paper
- embroidery hoop

## STITCHES USED

*For items embroidered with outlined flowers*
- back stitch
- straight stitch
- French knot
- fern stitch

*For items embroidered with solid flowers*
- satin stitch
- French knot
- chain stitch

For full details on stitches, see pages 132–7.

## TECHNIQUES

For full practical information, see pages 129–31.

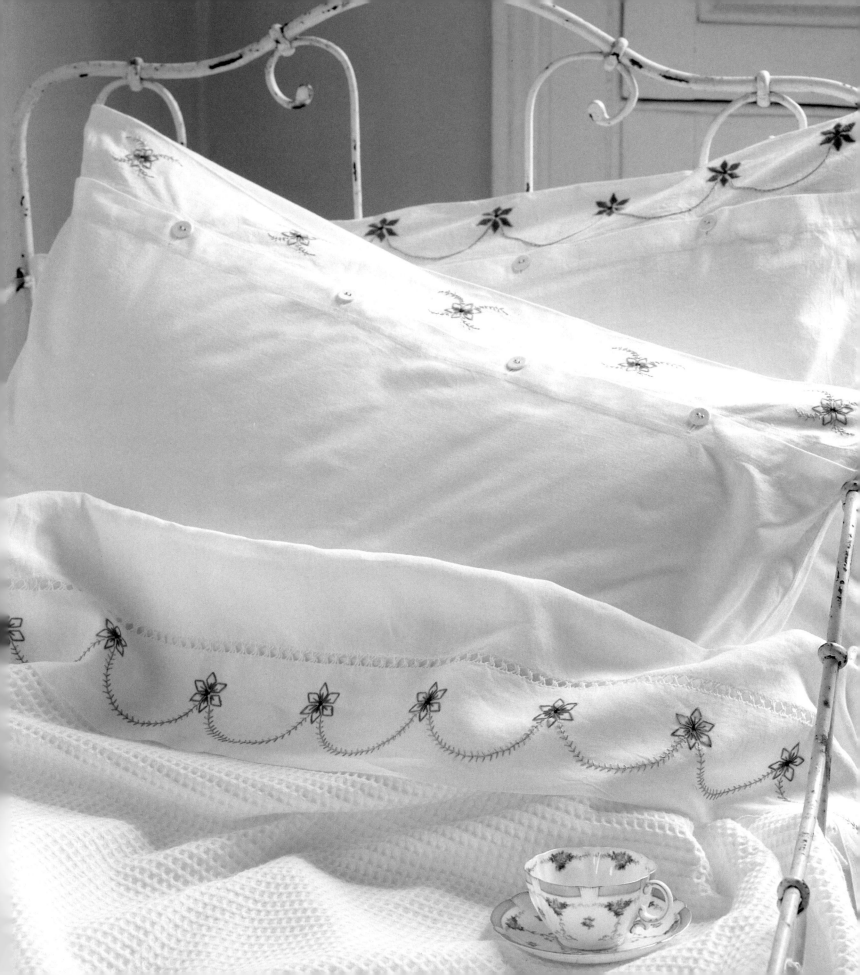

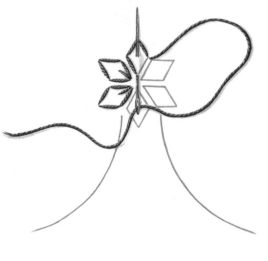

*1. To embroider the flowers for the sheet, first outline each petal with four large back stitches, finishing with one straight stitch in the centre.*
*2. Embroider each scallop in fern stitch.*

**1**

**2**

### To work the sheet with outlined flowers

Enlarge the template opposite to 125% on a photocopier. Using dressmaker's carbon paper, transfer the template onto your sheet as instructed below.

Place the first flower in the centre of the top edge of the sheet and continue to repeat the flower and scallop motif on either side of this first flower, working out towards both side edges of the sheet. This will ensure that the border pattern finishes symmetrically at the sheet edges.

The entire design is worked with three strands of thread. First, stitch the petals in pink, starting at the centre point of each one. Outline each petal with four large back stitches, and then work one straight stitch in the centre of each petal (see 1 above). In the centre of each flower embroider three French knots in red. Following the line of the scallop, work fern stitch from one flower to the next in green (see 2 above and top right of photograph opposite).

### To work the pillowcase with outlined flowers

Enlarge the flower head only of the template opposite to 110% on a photocopier. Using a tape measure and sewing pins, plan the placement of the flower heads along the edge of the pillowcase. I positioned each of my motifs 15cm (6in) apart. For a denser pattern, position the flowers closer together. Using dressmaker's carbon paper, transfer the template to your pillowcase. Stitch the flowers as for the sheet.

To create the curling stems (see top left of photograph opposite), draw freehand with a pencil a short curve on either side of each flower, or, if it helps, trace around something of a suitable size. Work the stems in fern stitch as for the sheet.

### To work the pillowcase with solid flowers

Following the instructions for the sheet border, transfer the template opposite along the edge of the pillowcase.

The flower petals and the scallop are worked with three strands of thread and the French knots with six. Embroider the petals in satin stitch, working the stitches horizontally (see centre of the photograph on the right). In the centre of each flower work just one French knot. Finally, following the line of the scallop, work chain stitch from one flower to the next.

**To work the buttons (outlined and solid)**
Enlarge or reduce the flower head of the template below to fit the button to be covered. Using dressmaker's carbon paper, transfer the template several times onto the fabric pieces, depending on the number of buttons to be covered. Leave a suitable gap between the motifs to allow for cutting out.

Stitch the outlined flowers as for the sheet, or the solid flowers as for the second pillowcase. If you are using very small buttons, reduce the number of strands to two or even one.

Make up the buttons according to the instructions given with the button-covering kit.

TEMPLATE

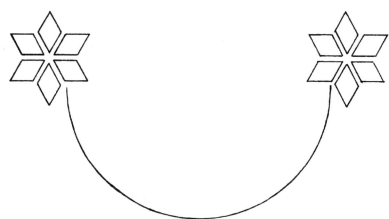

COLOUR GUIDE

| Pink | Red | Green |
| 3607 | 606 | 704 |

# SCATTERED LEAVES

This design is made up of three different leaf motifs – oak, maple and horse chestnut – all chosen for their strong and interesting shapes. I have used bright shades in the ever-popular combinations of blue and white and green and white, which give a feeling of freshness and are reminiscent of spring.

*BELOW: The corner of a coloured napkin is embellished with two oak leaves. In contrast to those on the tablecloth, these leaves are finely detailed, with extra veins and stems.*

For the tablecloth the leaves are scattered across the fabric in a very informal way, but they would look equally effective arranged in a row along the edges of the tablecloth to form a border. Another option is to enlarge one of the leaf designs to a dramatic scale so that it fills the front of a cushion cover. In this case, six strands of embroidery thread, rather than the three needed for the tablecloth, would be required.

## MATERIALS

- DMC stranded cotton in the following colours:
  fresh green 704
  lime green 3819
  turquoise 913
  cream 712 (*coloured napkins only*)

  Quantities depend on the size of the tablecloth and how densely scattered you want the leaves to be. For my 90cm (36in) square cloth with 15 leaves (five each of the three different shapes), one skein of each colour was sufficient. One extra skein of fresh green was required for the border pattern.

- plain cotton or linen tablecloth or, if you prefer to make your own, cotton or linen fabric
- napkins or fabric to match the tablecloth
- crewel (embroidery) needle size 6
- dressmaker's carbon paper
- embroidery hoop

## STITCHES USED

fern stitch
back stitch
stem stitch
blanket stitch
straight stitch
chain stitch

For full details on stitches, see pages 132–7.

## TECHNIQUES

For full practical information on methods used in this project, see pages 129–31.

*LEFT: A plain linen tablecloth is transformed when embroidered with a few scattered leaves and a simple zig-zag border.*

## MAPLE LEAF

Using fresh green and starting at the top of the stem, embroider blanket stitch round the outline of the maple leaf. The rest of the leaf is worked in stem stitch – single rows for the leaf veins and a double row for the stem.

## OAK LEAF

Using turquoise, embroider the central vein of the leaf in back stitch. Every few stitches work a pair of straight stitches at an angle to create the side veins, which should correspond with the protruding parts of the leaf (see 1 below). Complete the oak leaf by working the outline in chain stitch.

When all the leaves are embroidered, work a zig-zag row of straight stitches along the edge of the tablecloth in fresh green (see 2 opposite).

### To work the tablecloth

On a photocopier, enlarge the oak leaf template to 120%, the horse chestnut leaf to 200% and the maple leaf to 135%. Make several copies of each and roughly cut round them to get rid of the excess paper. Lay the tablecloth flat on the floor, or drape it over the table it is intended for, and scatter the copies over it. When you are satisfied with the arrangement, pin the copies temporarily in place. Transfer the leaves onto their marked positions on the fabric using dressmaker's carbon paper.

The entire design is worked using three strands of thread. Embroider each leaf as follows.

### HORSE CHESTNUT LEAF

Using lime green, work fern stitch for the veins of the horse chestnut leaf. Start at the top of each leaf segment with one back stitch and then continue down towards the centre, enlarging the stitch as the segment widens and then reducing it as the segment narrows (see photograph opposite). When it becomes too narrow at the centre of the leaf to work fern stitch, finish with one or two back stitches. Outline each of the leaves in stem stitch and then finish the design with two rows of stem stitch for each leaf stem.

*1. Back stitch is used for the central vein of the oak leaf, while angled straight stitches create the side veins.*
*2. A zig-zag line of straight stitches along the edge of the tablecloth shows another way of using this simple stitch.*

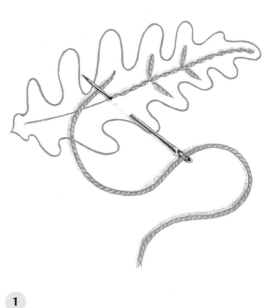

1

## COLOUR GUIDE

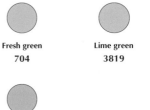

Fresh green
704

Lime green
3819

Turquoise
913

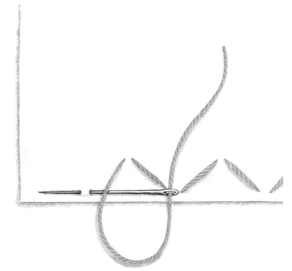

**2**

### To work the napkin

For this you need two oak leaf templates, one the same size as the original, the other enlarged on a photocopier to 120%. Referring to the photograph on page 22, add a stem about 3–4cm (1¼–1½in) long to each leaf, and inside the leaf add diagonal lines radiating out from the central vein. Place the two templates together and transfer them onto the corner of the napkin using dressmaker's carbon paper.

The entire design is worked with three strands of thread. Using either cream embroidery thread on a coloured napkin or one of the green threads on a white napkin, work stem stitch along the diagonal leaf veins. Embroider chain stitch down the centre of each leaf and on down the stem. Finally, complete the leaf outlines, still working in chain stitch.

# SUMMER SPRIGS

Sprigs are dainty single flowers, each with a short stem and one or two leaves. Traditionally, they were printed onto fabrics in irregular patterns, as though strewn across the cloth. These demure fabrics, known as sprigged cottons, were immensely popular for summer dresses throughout the eighteenth and nineteenth centuries.

My sprigged pillowcase is a homage to these fabrics, informal yet feminine. By contrast, the crisp linen handkerchief features just one sprig, revealed in all its delicate beauty.

*ABOVE: A plain white linen handkerchief is the perfect foil for a single dainty sprig in full bloom. OPPOSITE: The same sprig enlarged and randomly scattered over a prettily trimmed square pillowcase.*

## MATERIALS

- DMC stranded embroidery cotton in the following colours:
    - deep pink 309
    - yellow 3820
    - pale pink 3779
    - mid pink 335
    - leaf green 470
    - olive green 3051

For the pillowcase, one skein of each colour is sufficient. For the handkerchiefs, one skein of each colour will work ten or more sprigs.

*For the square pillowcase*
- 70 x 140cm (27½ x 56in) square of white cotton or linen fabric, or ready-made square pillowcase
- 55cm (22in) square pillow
- 2.3m (2¼yd) lace trimming
- 30cm (12in) ribbon or cotton tape

*For the handkerchief*
- ready-made fine white handkerchief or, if you prefer to make your own, fine cotton fabric

*For both projects*
- set square
- tracing paper
- crewel (embroidery) needle size 6 for the pillowcase, 9 for the handkerchief
- dressmaker's carbon paper
- embroidery hoop

## STITCHES USED

satin stitch

French knot

stem stitch

straight stitch

For full details on stitches, see pages 132–7.

## TECHNIQUES

For full practical information, see pages 129–31.

**To work the pillowcase**

If you are making your own pillowcase, use a set square and a ruler to mark out a 55cm (22in) square on the cotton or linen fabric. Add a 2.5cm (1in) seam allowance all round and cut out.

Trace or photocopy the template 12 times (some of these could be reversed). Cut out these copies very roughly (to get rid of excess paper) and space them evenly across the fabric square or pillowcase. Be careful not to place the sprigs too near the edge

RIGHT: To radiate the deep pink stitches evenly from the centre of each flower head, it helps to embroider a few guide stitches first. These straight stitches, one for each petal, will blend in easily with the satin stitches that follow.

of the fabric, as they might get taken up into the seam. To prevent the design from looking too rigid and regular, alter the angle of each flower sprig so that they are pointing in different directions (refer to the photograph on page 27). Once you are satisfied with the arrangement of your flowers, transfer them onto the fabric or pillowcase using dressmaker's carbon paper.

The entire design is worked with three strands of thread. Refer to the template below for the direction in which the stitches should run. The heavier lines indicate stem stitch. Start by stitching the centre of the flower (the area surrounding the yellow stamens) in deep pink, using radiating satin stitch. To achieve an even effect, it helps to work a few straight or guide stitches first (see illustration top right). Next work a cluster of yellow French knots in the centre of each flower to form the stamens.

Work the petals in satin stitch, embroidering two petals in pale pink and the rest in mid pink. If you wish, vary the arrangement of the darker and paler pinks to prevent the flowers from looking unnaturally identical.

Work the hatched area of each leaf in satin stitch and the leaf outlines in stem stitch. Finally, work the stems with two rows of stem stitch, one slightly shorter than the other to give a tapered effect.

**To make up the pillowcase**
For the backing, mark out two rectangles on the remaining fabric, one measuring 40 x 55cm (16 x 22in) and the other 15 x 55cm (6 x 22in). Add a 2.5cm (1in) seam allowance all round and cut out. Place the two pieces right sides and long edges

together and, using a sewing machine or small back stitches, join along one long edge with a 2.5cm (1in) seam, leaving enough seam open in the middle to insert the pillow. Press the seam open.

With right sides facing, pin and stitch the embroidery to the backing fabric, using a 2.5cm (1in) seam. Snip across the corners to reduce bulk and turn the case right side out. Sew the lace edging all around the pillowcase, slip stitching along the seam edge. To close the opening at the back, cut the ribbon or tape in two and sew one length on each side to tie in a bow after the pillow has been inserted.

**To work the handkerchief**
Reduce the template (left) to 85% on a photocopier. Using dressmaker's carbon paper, transfer the design onto the corner of the handkerchief.

The entire design is worked with two strands of thread. Following the embroidery instructions for the pillowcase, work in exactly the same way.

TEMPLATE

Deep pink
309

Yellow
3820

Pale pink
3779

Mid pink
335

Leaf green
470

Olive green
3051

# STYLIZED BLOOMS

*While the petals and leaves of small flowers are well suited to dense stitching, such as the Summer Sprigs embroidered in satin stitch (see page 26), bold, stylized flowers are too large for solid blocks of colour. They tend to work better with open stitching and patterns, where plenty of background fabric is visible. This eight-petalled bloom can be worked in four different ways, and can be used either on small bags or in a grid pattern on a cushion cover. If you like, you could add extra textural detail by sewing a button in the centre of each bloom.*

*The projects shown here illustrate how the appearance of one simple motif can vary depending on the type of stitches used and the way in which they are arranged.*

*ABOVE: A cushion cover is divided into a grid with lines of chain stitch; each alternate square is filled with a bloom.*
*OPPOSITE: A single button embellishes an embroidered bloom on a simple bag.*

## MATERIALS

- DMC stranded embroidery cotton in the following colours:
  cream 712 (*fly stitch bag, French knot bag and cushion cover only*)
  toffee 436 (*chain stitch bag only*)
  beige 738 (*French knot bag only*)
- DMC Coton Perlé No. 5 in cream 712 (*blanket stitch bag only*)

One skein of thread is more than sufficient to complete one bloom for a bag. Three skeins are sufficient for the whole cushion.

*For the bags*
- 50cm (20in) square of linen or cotton fabric for each bag

For the blanket stitch bag, which is embroidered with a thicker thread, it is important to choose a loose-woven fabric that will allow the needle and thread to pass through easily.

*For the cushion cover*
- 50cm (20in) square of unbleached loose-woven linen fabric, or ready-made cushion cover
- set square
- tailor's chalk
- tracing paper
- 35cm (14in) zip
- 40cm (16in) square cushion pad
- 50cm (20in) square of linen fabric for backing

*For all projects*
- crewel (embroidery) needle size 5
- dressmaker's carbon paper
- embroidery hoop

## STITCHES USED

| | |
|---|---|
| blanket stitch | chain stitch |
| fly stitch | French knot |
| stem stitch | |

(The blanket stitch and chain stitch bags use just one stitch each, while the fly stitch and French knot bags also use stem stitch. The cushion uses all the stitches.)
For full details on stitches, see pages 132–7.

## TECHNIQUES

For full information, see pages 129–31.

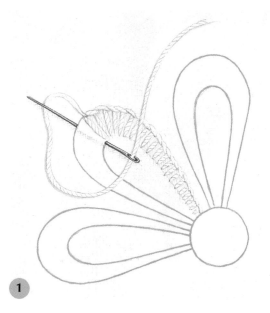

## To work the chain stitch bag

Enlarge the bloom template on page 34 to 140% on a photocopier. Using dressmaker's carbon paper, transfer the design onto the fabric (see blanket stitch bag for positioning).

The entire design is worked in chain stitch with six strands of thread for the outer edge of the petals and the centre and three strands for the inner edge of the petals. Begin stitching each petal at the centre, following the pattern lines up, round and back again to the centre. Use larger stitches for the outer edge and the centre.

When all the petals are complete, work a circle of chain stitch in the centre of the flower, just touching the base of each petal (see 2 below).

## To work the blanket stitch bag

Enlarge the bloom template on page 34 to 140% on a photocopier. Using dressmaker's carbon paper, transfer the design onto one of the squares of linen fabric. I positioned my bloom so that the centre lay 14cm (5½in) from the bottom of the square and equidistant from both sides. This ensures the correct placement when the bag is made up.

The entire design is embroidered in blanket stitch with six strands of thread. Working from left to right and beginning each petal at the centre, start stitching, following the two working lines round and back to the centre. As the distance between these two lines widens to mark the thickening of the petals, so you will need to increase the length of the stitches (see 1 above).

When all the petals are complete, work a circle of blanket stitch in the centre of the flower.

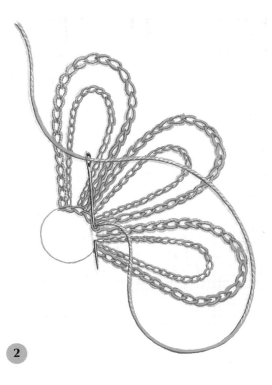

### To work the French knot bag

Enlarge the bloom template on page 34 to 140% on a photocopier. Using dressmaker's carbon paper, transfer the design onto the fabric (see blanket stitch bag for positioning).

Unless stated otherwise, six strands of thread are used. First work the outer edge of each petal in stem stitch, using cream thread. To give this line a thicker, twisted effect, pass the needle either side of the working line. Now work the inner pattern line of each petal, but this time use only three strands of thread. Continue to work in stem stitch, but this time pass the needle directly along the working line to achieve a finer line. Work two circles of stem stitch in the centre of the flower, leaving a gap between

**4**

them (see 3 below). Work a row of French knots in beige between the two lines that form the petals and between the two centre circles of the flower.

### To work the fly stitch bag

Enlarge the bloom template on page 34 to 140% on a photocopier. Using dressmaker's carbon paper, transfer the design onto the fabric (see blanket stitch bag for positioning).

The entire design is worked with six strands of thread. Work both outline edges of each petal in stem stitch. In the centre of each petal work a row of seven or eight fly stitches (see 4 above). Finish the flower with a circle of stem stitch in the centre.

### To make up the bags

For each bag, fold the fabric square in half, right sides together, so that the fold line passes vertically through the embroidery. Machine stitch a 2cm (¾in) seam down the long side. Press the seam, then flatten the bag so that the seam lies in the centre of the back. Now stitch a 2cm (¾in) seam along the

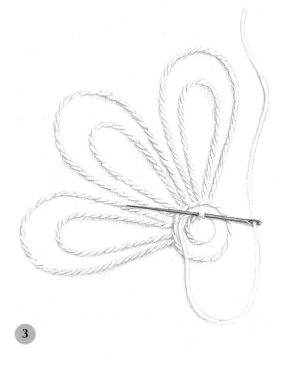

**3**

*3. French knot bag:*
*To achieve neat circles in the centre of the bloom, keep the stem stitches even in length and sloped at exactly the same angle to the line. This way the stitches of the inner circle will be smaller than those of the outer circle.*

*4. Fly stitch bag:*
*Down the centre of each petal work a series of fly stitches, one below the other. As the petal lines narrow, reduce the size of each stitch, but not the distance between them.*

square at 10, 20 and 30cm (4, 8 and 12in), thus dividing it into four rows of 10cm (4in) squares (refer to photograph left). Trace or photocopy the bloom template below and transfer it using dressmaker's carbon paper into every alternate square marked out on the fabric. This will give you eight blooms.

The entire design is worked with three strands of thread. Stitch the blooms as for the four bags, working each variation twice. Note that the French knot design has been simplified to suit the smaller scale: it now has only one centre circle. Work the dividing grid lines in chain stitch.

bottom of the bag and a 2cm (¾in) hem around the top. Turn the bag right side out. Fold the top 12.5cm (5in) to the inside and sew a row of top stitching around the top edge.

### To work the cushion cover

Using a set square and a ruler mark out a 40cm (16in) square on your loose-woven linen. Add on a 4.5cm (1¾in) seam and border allowance all round, then cut out. With tailor's chalk, draw three vertical and three horizontal lines within the marked-out

### To make up the cushion cover

For the backing fabric you will need to cut two pieces of matching linen, one measuring 49 x 18cm (19½ x 7¼in) and the other 49 x 35cm (19½ x 13¾in). Place the two pieces right sides together and with their long sides aligning. Using a sewing machine or small back stitches, join along the long edge with a 2cm (¾in) seam to form a 49cm (19½in) square. Make sure you leave enough seam open in the middle to accommodate the length of the zip. Press the seams flat. Pin, tack and then machine stitch the zip into position.

With right sides facing (and the zip open), pin and machine stitch the embroidered linen square to the backing linen, leaving a 2.5cm (1in) seam allowance all round. Snip across the corners to avoid a bulky finish and turn the cushion cover right side out. Press. Machine stitch a 2cm (¾in) border all round through both layers of fabric. Over this machine line work a line of chain stitch in order to create a frame for the design.

TEMPLATE

Toffee
436

# SPRAYS OF WILD FLOWERS

*BELOW AND OPPOSITE: A colourful spray of wild flowers adds the prettiest of touches to a plain cushion and tray cloth.*

Unlike a bouquet of flowers, which tends to be a rather formal arrangement, a spray is more natural, as though the flowers have been effortlessly bunched together. For my spray design I chose to use wild flowers, grasses and long stems for a summery, rustic look, and positioned the designs so that the flowers appear to spill casually over the front of a cushion and the corner of a tray cloth.

## MATERIALS

- DMC stranded embroidery cotton in the following colours for both projects:

    navy 791

    dark purple 553

    mid purple 554

    deep pink 3805

    mid pink 3607

    pale pink 3608

    yellow ochre 3821

    green 471

    *Additional colours for the cushion cover:*

    cream 3823

    pale purple 210

    orange 350

    bright yellow 743

    apple green 989

    dark lilac 3746

    mid lilac 340

    One skein of each colour is more than sufficient for both the cushion cover and tray cloth.

*For the cushion cover*

- 1m x 50cm (40 x 20in) of plain cotton or linen fabric, or a ready-made cushion cover
- 30cm (12in) zip
- 35cm (14in) cushion pad

*RIGHT: As you work long and short stitch round the outside edge of the flower, use the dotted line as a guide for the length of the short stitches. These should extend from the outside edge to just over the dotted line. The alternating long stitches should be roughly twice the length.*

TEMPLATE

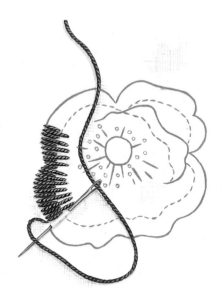

*For the tray cloth*

- 50cm (20in) of plain cotton or linen fabric, or a ready-made tray cloth

*For both projects*

- tracing paper
- set square
- crewel (embroidery) needle size 6
- dressmaker's carbon paper
- embroidery hoop

## STITCHES USED

long and short stitch

stem stitch

French knot

straight stitch

lazy daisy stitch

satin stitch

For full details on stitches, see pages 132–7.

## TECHNIQUES

For full information, see pages 129–31.

### To work the cushion cover

Using a set square and a ruler, mark out a 40cm (16in) square on your fabric. Add a 2cm (¾in) seam allowance all round and cut out. Enlarge the large template opposite to 220% on a photocopier. Using dressmaker's carbon paper, transfer the design onto the fabric, making sure the pattern is placed in the centre of the fabric square.

Refer to the photograph on page 41 for use of colour. Start stitching in the centre, working the largest flower first. Embroider long and short stitch round the outside edge and part of the inside of the flower, using the dotted line as a guide for the length of the short stitches (see illustration above). Use stem stitch to outline the outer edges of the long and short stitch; this will help to define the shape. Work a

## To make up the cushion cover

For the backing fabric you will need to mark out two pieces of matching fabric, one piece 40 x 15cm (16 x 6in) and the other 40 x 25cm (16 x 10in). Add a 2cm (¾in) seam allowance all round and cut out. Place the two pieces together and, using a sewing machine or small back stitches, join along one long edge with a 2cm (¾in) seam, leaving enough seam open in the middle for the length of the zip. Press the seam flat. Pin, tack and then machine stitch the zip into position.

With right sides facing and zip open, pin and machine stitch the embroidery to the backing fabric, allowing a 2cm (¾in) seam all round. Snip across the corners to avoid a bulky finish and turn the cushion cover to the right side. Press. Machine stitch a 1.5cm (½in) border all round through both layers of fabric. Insert the cushion pad.

central clump of French knots, then around these work more French knots, but this time scattered, and some radiating straight stitches.

The petals of the remaining flowers are worked in lazy daisy stitch. For the smallest flowers, which are randomly coloured in three shades of purple, work one lazy daisy stitch for each petal and one French knot in the centre. The whole cornflowers are also randomly coloured, this time in two shades of lilac. Work three lazy daisy stitches for each petal and, in the centre of the flowers, a few French knots. For the daisies work one lazy daisy stitch for each petal and some French knots in the centre.

Work the stems in stem stitch, the sprays of grass in lazy daisy and the blades of grass in satin stitch.

## To work the tray cloth

The wild flower spray for the tray cloth is made up of just a few elements taken from the whole cushion design. Either trace the small template on page 38 or, working freehand or using tracing paper, compose a simple arrangement of flowers and leaves, taking the shapes from the large template on page 39. Using dressmaker's carbon paper, transfer the finished pattern onto one corner of the tray cloth. Be careful not to place the motif too near the edge of the cloth, or you will not be able to mount the fabric into the embroidery hoop.

Colour and stitch the design exactly as for the cushion, then repeat on the opposite corner of the tray cloth.

COLOUR GUIDE

 Mid pink
3607

Deep pink
3805

Pale pink
3608

Yellow ochre
3821

Navy
791

Pale purple
210

Mid purple
554

Dark purple
553

 Mid lilac
340

Dark lilac
3746

Orange
350

Bright yellow
743

Cream
3823

Green
471

Apple green
989

# Nature's Harvest

WHEN I WAS LOOKING FOR images to translate into embroidery for this book, it was often the shape of an object or a flower that inspired me. With the emphasis on the outline of an image, rather than on the finer detail or colouring, stitches could be used quite sparingly – a simple line of chain stitch was enough to convey the elegance of a water jug, while one lazy daisy stitch made the perfect petal. Sometimes, as in the case of two of the projects in this chapter, richness of colour was the inspiration. The irregular outlines of summer fruits and vegetables, such as lemons, strawberries, peas and carrots, are filled and shaded in with solid colour and stitches, in the same way that an artist uses a pencil and brush to draw and paint. Working in this way gives enormous scope for playing with different stitches, as almost any embroidery stitch can be adapted for use as a filling stitch. I chose long and short stitch, the classic stitch for shading, because I love the way the stitches blend into one another to give a beautifully smooth and solid field of colour. If the idea of so many stitches appears daunting, particularly if the motif is repeated in a row to form a decorative band, the motif can simply be outlined, as demonstrated by the cherries on the picnic cutlery holder on the right.

*LEFT: Cherry motifs are arranged in an orderly pattern along the edge of a cutlery bag.*
*OPPOSITE: Golden wheat sheaves tumble over a linen basket cloth.*

# BREAKFAST COCKEREL

*BELOW AND OPPOSITE:*
*A stylized cockerel in bold*
*colours is equally effective on*
*its own or in a repeat pattern.*

*The cockerel napkin is an excellent project for the embroidery novice to tackle. It introduces three of the most widely used stitches: stem, satin and French knot. In addition, the cockerel has been pared down to the simplest of outlines, with just enough detail to give it interest. For the curtain border, where the cockerel is used to form a repeat pattern, no extra skills are required – only more time.*

## MATERIALS

- DMC stranded embroidery cotton in the following colours:
  - blue 798
  - red 666
  - yellow 973
  - cream 3823 (*blue napkin only*)

  One skein of each colour will be sufficient to embroider six napkins; the curtain with six cockerels requires two skeins of blue and one each of yellow and red.
- fine cotton or linen napkins
- ready-made cream cotton or linen curtains, or loose-woven cream linen sufficient to make up a curtain to the required size
- crewel (embroidery) needle size 7 for the napkin, size 5 for the curtain
- dressmaker's carbon paper
- embroidery hoop

## STITCHES USED

  stem stitch
  satin stitch
  French knot
  straight stitch (*napkins only*)
  fly stitch (*curtain border only*)
For full details on stitches, see pages 132–7.

TEMPLATE

### TECHNIQUES

For full practical information on methods used in this project, see pages 129–31.

### To work the napkins

Enlarge the template above to 120% on a photocopier. Using dressmaker's carbon paper, transfer the template onto the corner of a napkin. Be careful not to place the cockerel too close to the corner of the napkin, or you will not be able to mount it in the embroidery hoop.

The entire design is worked with three strands of thread. Refer to the photograph on page 47 for the colours used. Start by stitching the outline and the body and tail markings of the cockerel in stem stitch (the direction of your stitches is unimportant). Work the comb, beak and wattle in satin stitch. Work one French knot for the cockerel's eye and three straight stitches for the feet.

### To work the curtain border

Enlarge the template above to 185% on a photocopier. Using a tape measure and sewing pins, plan the placement of the cockerels along the bottom edge of the curtain fabric. I positioned each of my motifs at 15cm (6in) intervals, measuring from the feet of one cockerel to the next, and 7.5cm (3in) from the bottom. This latter measurement includes a 5cm (2in) hem allowance for making up the curtains. For a denser border pattern, position the cockerels closer together. Use dressmaker's carbon paper to transfer the pattern. Do not extend the border too near the edges of the curtain; you will need to leave 5cm (2in) for each side hem.

Stitch the cockerel as for the napkin, but make the following changes: work all stem stitch with six rather than three strands of thread; work the feet in stem stitch rather than straight stitch, and embroider the eye with three French knots.

### To make up the curtain

Turn under double side hems of 2.5cm (1in) and a double bottom hem of 2.5cm (1in) and neatly hand stitch them in place. Work a row of fly stitches along the bottom of the curtain in red using three strands of thread (see illustration below). Finally, attach the heading tape of your choice to the top of the curtain and draw up the gathering threads to make the required width.

*RIGHT: The curtain hem is decorated with a row of fly stitches. Working from left to right, pick up a diagonal stitch, with the needle point over the loop. Then make a small vertical stitch to hold the loop in place.*

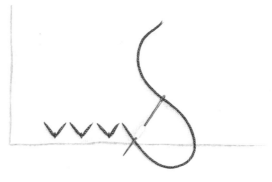

# GOLDEN WHEAT SHEAVES

Wheat is the ancient symbol of harvest as well as prosperity and fertility, and is strongly associated with the countryside and a rural way of life. A field of golden wheat sheaves arranged in stooks is a timeless and evocative scene, and to reinforce this image I chose embroidery threads and fabrics in colours similar to those seen at harvest time – warm shades of gold, yellow, and brown. In keeping with the rustic theme I embroidered the wheat sheaves randomly over the tablecloth so that they look natural, as though I had no hand in their placement. By contrast, those on the bread basket cloth form a neat border, the sheaves naturally complementing the basket's contents.

*RIGHT: A loosely woven linen cloth embroidered with sprays of wheat sheaves adorns a country kitchen table. OPPOSITE: The same design is used to decorate the edge of a bread basket cloth.*

## MATERIALS

- DMC stranded embroidery cotton in the following colours:
  gold 783
  toffee 729
  sand 676
  Quantities depend on the size of tablecloth used and also on the density of pattern. For my 90cm (36in) square cloth with 15 wheat sheaf sprays, two skeins of each colour were sufficient. For the border on the bread basket cloth, one skein of each colour was plenty.
- natural-coloured linen tablecloth or loose-woven natural-coloured linen
- basket cloth (I used a very large napkin in fine linen with a drawn-thread border)
- tracing paper
- crewel (embroidery) needle size 5 for the tablecloth, size 7 for the basket cloth
- dressmaker's carbon paper
- embroidery hoop

## STITCHES USED

lazy daisy stitch
stem stitch
running stitch
For full details on stitches, see pages 132–7.

## TECHNIQUES

For full practical information on the methods used in this project, refer to Techniques on pages 129-31.

COLOUR GUIDE

Gold
783

Toffee
729

Sand
676

TEMPLATE

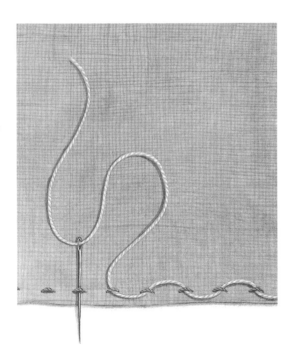

LEFT: *For the tablecloth hem decoration, first work a line of running stitches. Bring a thread in a contrasting colour through at one end of the line and pass it in and out of the stitches without picking up any fabric. This thread passes through the material only at the beginning and end of its length.*

## To work the tablecloth

Enlarge the template above to 175% on a photocopier. To help you plan the placement of your pattern, copy this enlarged motif several times. Very roughly cut around these copies to get rid of the excess paper. Lay the tablecloth flat on the floor, or drape it over the table it is intended for, and randomly arrange the copies of the wheat sheaves (see photograph on page 50). When you are satisfied with the arrangement, pin the copies temporarily to mark their position. Using dressmaker's carbon paper, transfer the pattern.

The entire design is worked with six strands of thread. Refer to the photograph on page 51 for the use of colour. The ears of wheat are worked in lazy daisy and their stems in stem stitch. Continue working in stem stitch for the wheat blades, but this time alter the angle so that the needle passes from one side of the blade to the other; this gives a thicker, twisted effect. To widen the blade, increase the angle of the stitches as you work progressively down it.

To decorate the hem of the tablecloth, first embroider a row of well-spaced running stitches along the edge, then weave a contrasting colour in and out of these stitches (see illustration above). Be careful not to pull the thread too tight.

## To work the bread basket cloth

Trace the template above. Using a tape measure and sewing pins, plan the placement of the wheat sheaves along the edge of your bread basket cloth (see photograph opposite). To prevent the design from looking too regular, alter the angle of the motifs so that they are pointing in slightly different directions. Work the wheat sheaves as for the tablecloth, but use only three strands of thread instead of six to achieve a finer result.

If your bread basket cloth does not already have a border pattern, you might like to add the same border pattern to the edge of your cloth as used for the tablecloth, or a row of fly stitches as used for the cockerel curtain border (see page 48).

# SUMMER FRUIT

These jug covers have each been embroidered with a different summer fruit. The lusciousness of the fruit is emphasized by the richness of colouring and the solid stitching – mainly satin stitch. For both decorative and practical reasons each cover has been trimmed with beads; the weight of these helps to hold the covers down over the jugs.

In contrast, the picnic cutlery holder (below left), decoratively edged with outlined cherries, shows how a design can be adapted. A single cherry has been taken from the template and repeated in a row. To prevent the design from looking too regular, the angle of every alternate cherry is reversed, so the stalks point in opposite directions.

*BELOW: Perfect for summer picnics, a canvas cutlery holder is embroidered with a simple row of cherries. Each cherry is outlined and highlighted with stem stitch, while satin stitch completes each stalk.*

## MATERIALS

- DMC stranded embroidery cotton in the following colours:

  *For the strawberry*
    bright red 666
    dark red 321
    pink 3705
    cream 712
    pale green 471
    dark green 470

  *For the cherries*
    scarlet 304
    plum red 815
    dark red 321
    cream 712
    orange 349
    green 471

  *For the lemon*
    cream 3823
    mid yellow 726
    pale yellow 727

  For all three fruits, one skein of each colour will work several jug covers.

- white cotton fabric, enough for a 22cm (8¾in) square for each cover, or to the size of your choice
- small beads (see instructions below for quantities and colours, but do not feel you have to stick to this colour scheme)
- set square
- tracing paper
- crewel (embroidery) needle size 6
- dressmaker's carbon paper
- embroidery hoop

## STITCHES USED

satin stitch
long and short stitch
straight stitch (*lemon only*)
back stitch (*lemon and cherries only*)
French knot (*strawberry only*)
stem stitch (*cherries only*)
running stitch
For full details on stitches, see pages 132–7.

## TECHNIQUES

For full practical information on the methods used in this project, refer to Techniques on pages 129–31.

ABOVE AND LEFT: Jugs of cooling summer drinks are draped with beaded covers embroidered with fruits of the season – a strawberry, a lemon and a bunch of ripe cherries.

*1. Working from right to left, embroider a line of long and short stitch along the bottom edge of the strawberry and two-thirds of the way up the left side. The short stitches must not extend beyond the dotted line, while the long stitches should, ready to blend with the next row of colour. 2. Shading with two or more colours: until a colour within a particular area is finished with, leave the needle threaded, but put to one side.*

## To work the strawberry

Using a set square and a ruler, mark out a 20cm (8in) square. Add a 2cm (¾in) hemming allowance all round and cut out. Trace the strawberry template on page 58 and use dressmaker's carbon paper to transfer it onto the middle of the fabric square.

The entire design is worked with three strands of thread. Work in long and short stitch as follows. With bright red, stitch a line of long and short stitches along the bottom and up the left side of the strawberry (see 1 above). Work next to these stitches an area in dark red, as indicated by the dotted line on the template, and, also in dark red, the dotted area along the top edge. In the oval dotted area to the right, work in pink. Embroider the rest of the strawberry in bright red. When all the long and short stitch is completed, work French knots in cream at random over the strawberry, scattering them more sparsely as you work downwards (see photograph on page 55). Alternating the use of the two different greens, work the stem and leaves in satin stitch, placing the stitches across the leaf or stem shape.

Hem the cover with running stitch in bright red. Sew one red bead at each corner of the square and nine evenly spaced along each edge.

## To work the cherries

Mark and cut out your fabric as for the strawberry cover. Trace the cherry template on page 58 and use dressmaker's carbon paper to transfer it onto the centre of the fabric square.

The entire design is worked with three strands of thread. Stitch one cherry at a time, starting with the central cherry, and working in long and short stitch (see 2 below). Embroider from the bottom of the cherry upwards. Rather than completing one area of colour at a time, work horizontally from side to side across each cherry. Use several needles threaded at once, one for each colour. When a colour or colours are not in use, simply put the needle(s) and thread(s) to one side until required.

The left side edge of the first cherry is worked in scarlet, which blends into an area of plum red, as

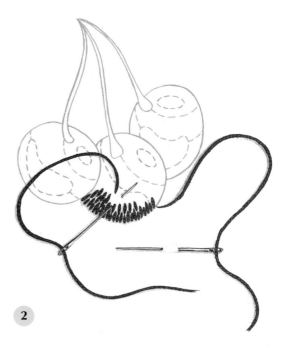

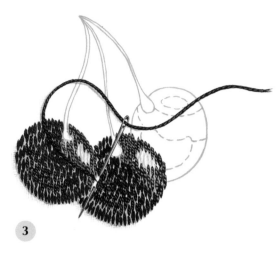

**3**

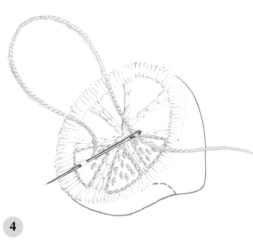

**4**

*3. To help define the outline of the first cherry so it does not blend with the second, work a line of small back stitches along the overlap.*

*4. For the flesh of each lemon segment, work short straight stitches. Arrange these in lines radiating out from the centre.*

indicated by the dotted line. Down the centre of the cherry is an area of dark red and to the right, surrounding the small highlight of cream, an area of orange. Shade the left-hand cherry in the same way, working a line of back stitch in plum red along the line where the two cherries overlap (see 3 above). Stitch the remaining cherry, again working a line of back stitch where it meets the central cherry. Embroider the stems in stem stitch, starting at the top of each stem and finishing at the base with a few satin stitches.

Hem the cover with running stitch in bright red. Sew on one green and two red beads at each corner.

**To work the lemon**

Mark and cut out your fabric as for the strawberry cover. Trace the lemon wedge template on page 58 and use dressmaker's carbon paper to transfer it onto the middle of the fabric square.

The entire design is worked with three strands of thread. Start stitching with cream, working the lemon pith first. Embroider the outer circle of pith in satin stitch, radiating the stitches outwards, and then fill the narrow areas of pith between each segment with long and short stitches. Outline each segment

with back stitch in mid yellow then fill each one with short straight stitches (see 4 above). Completely cover the peel of the lemon with long and short stitches, working one-third in pale yellow and the other two-thirds in mid yellow.

Hem the jug cover with running stitch in mid yellow. Sew one green bead at each corner of the square and four evenly spaced white beads along each of the edges.

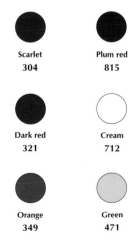

**COLOUR GUIDE**

| | |
|---|---|
| Scarlet 304 | Plum red 815 |
| Dark red 321 | Cream 712 |
| Orange 349 | Green 471 |

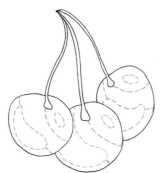

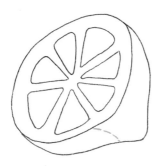

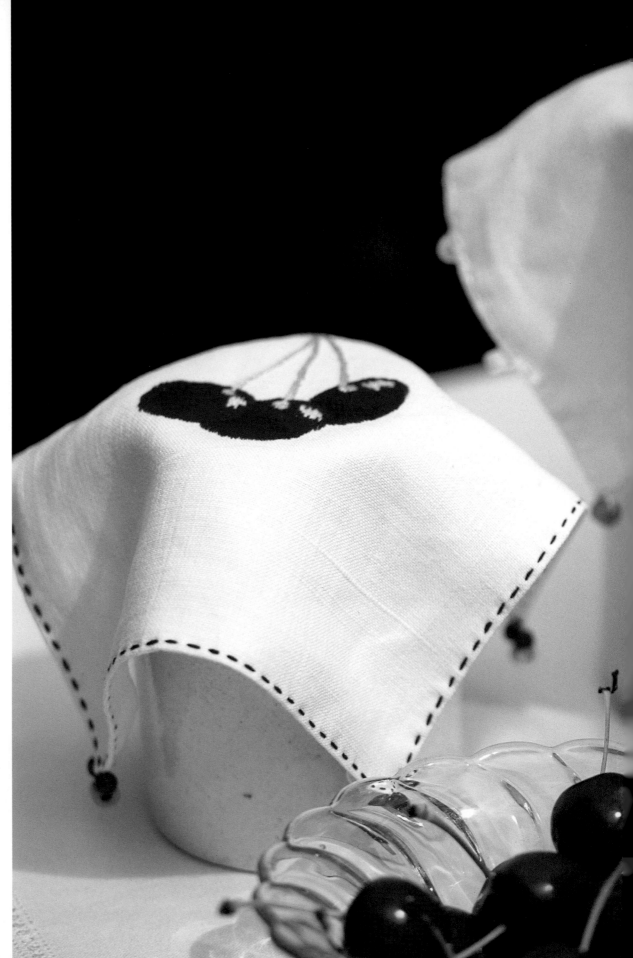

# GARDEN VEGETABLES

A few basic embroidery stitches are sometimes all that is necessary to convey the image of a beautiful flower. A vegetable, however, is less delicate in shape and requires more attention to detail to prevent it looking crude. The designs of both the bunch of carrots and the pea-pods use a palette of natural colours, which is one of the first things you notice about them, along with the density of their stitching. Both images are completely covered in stitches, nearly all of which are long and short stitch. This is the most widely used of all close filling stitches, largely because it is so quick and easy, and is ideal for the gradual blending of colour, like shading with coloured crayons. It is this blending that gives the images a three-dimensional effect.

*BELOW AND OPPOSITE:*
*A picnic basket is lined with*
*a cloth richly embroidered*
*with a bunch of carrots, while*
*another cloth, decorated with*
*two ripe pea-pods, holds*
*freshly picked peas. The*
*realistic colouring of both*
*designs is achieved with*
*long and short stitch.*

## MATERIALS

- DMC stranded embroidery cotton in the following colours:

  *For the pea-pods*
  > dark green 987
  > cream 712
  > light green 471
  > mid green 988
  > pale green 472

  *For the carrots*
  > dark green 367
  > light green 368
  > bright orange 946
  > dark orange 720
  > mid orange 721
  > cream 712
  > pale orange 722

  One skein of each colour is more than enough for both projects.
- cream cotton or linen tablecloth for each project, or sufficient cotton or linen fabric
- crewel (embroidery) needle size 6
- dressmaker's carbon paper
- embroidery hoop

## STITCHES USED

> satin stitch
> long and short stitch
> straight stitch
> stem stitch

For full details on stitches, see pages 132–7.

TEMPLATE

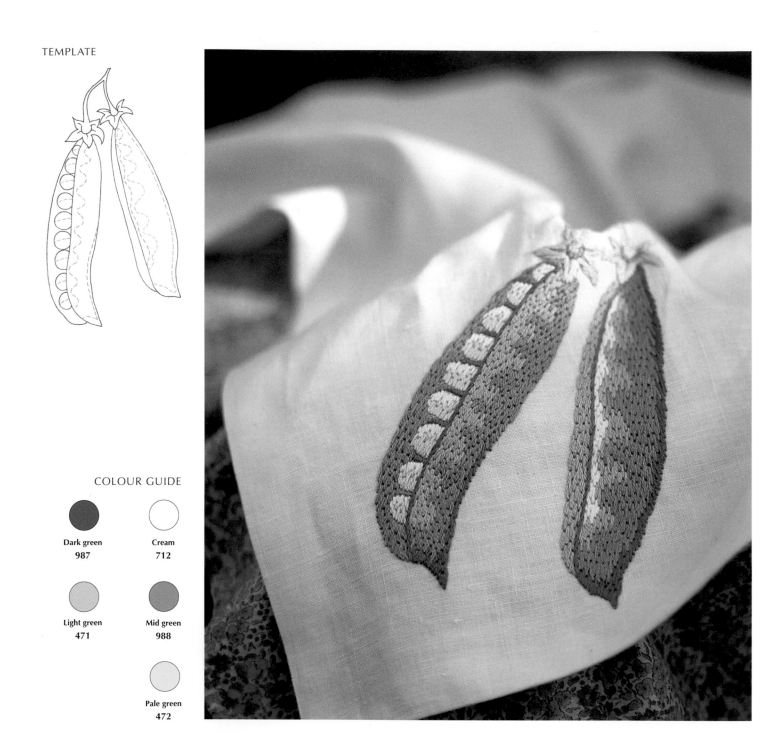

COLOUR GUIDE

Dark green
987

Cream
712

Light green
471

Mid green
988

Pale green
472

## TECHNIQUES

For full practical information on the methods used in this project, refer to Techniques on pages 129–31.

### To work the pea-pods

Enlarge the pea-pods template opposite to 200% on a photocopier. Using dressmaker's carbon paper, transfer the design onto one corner of your cloth. Be careful not to place the motif too close to the corner of the cloth, or you will not be able to mount it in the embroidery hoop.

The entire design is worked with three strands of thread. Refer to the photographs for colour and stitch direction. Work the left-hand pea-pod first. With dark green, embroider a few satin stitches in between each pea (see illustration right). Now work in long and short stitch only. First shade the peas with cream and light green thread. Work the area to the left of the peas in mid green and the area to the right, up to the dotted wavy line, in pale green. At the base of the pod work a few stitches in dark green before extending this colour up the right-hand side of the pod, using the dotted line. Complete the rest of the pod in mid green. Down the centre of the motif, along the edge of the peas, work a row of stem stitches in dark green.

Next work the right-hand pea-pod. Embroider the left side of the pod in pale green. Moving to the right, highlight a small area down the length of the pod in cream and then stitch in pale green in the area indicated by the dotted lines. At the base of the pod and up its outer edge work a few stitches in dark green before completing the rest of the pod

in mid green. Down the centre of the pod work a row of stem stitches in dark green along the edge of the cream highlight.

With light green thread, stitch the pod stems in satin stitch, making the stitches at a slight angle rather than straight across the stem. Around the base of the stem embroider the pod tops or leaves in satin stitch, radiating the stitches outwards down the length of each leaf. Change to mid green thread and work one straight stitch in the centre of each leaf in the same direction, and then finish with a few tiny stem stitches round the base of the stem to define the shape.

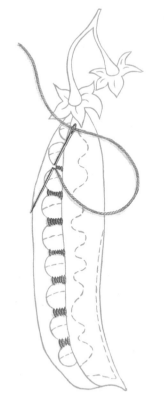

*LEFT: To help clarify the shape of each pea, embroider a few satin stitches in dark green in between them. Start from the centre and work outwards, keeping the stitches close together, until the space between each pea has been filled.*

RIGHT: *The carrot tops*
*or stems are diagonally*
*embroidered in dark green*
*satin stitch. Alter the*
*direction of the diagonal*
*with each stem.*

TEMPLATE

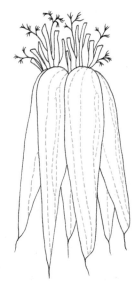

## To work the carrots

Enlarge the carrots template (left) to 220% on a photocopier. Using dressmaker's carbon paper, transfer the design onto one corner of your cloth.

The entire design is worked with three strands of thread. For all shading, the long and short stitches are made horizontally across the carrot, unlike those of the pea-pods, which are made vertically (see photographs on pages 62 and 65). I chose to work the tops first and then the carrots themselves, but the order is unimportant.

Using dark green, embroider the carrot tops in satin stitch, working diagonally across each stem (see illustration right). Change the thread to light green and work the feathery leaves in straight stitch and their stems in stem stitch.

Embroidering the central (and only whole) carrot first, work a line of long and short stitches down the left side of the carrot in bright orange. Moving to the right, work a line in dark orange, then mid orange before working the area indicated by a dotted line in cream. Finish the carrot in pale orange. Embroider the two larger carrots on either side of this central carrot in the same way, but work smaller stitches to suit their narrower size. The three remaining carrots are worked in dark and pale orange only.

When all shading with long and short stitch is finished, outline the left-hand edge of each carrot with a line of stem stitch in the same colour used for the first line of shading. Start at the top of the carrot and work downwards, extending the stitches to form a carrot tail (see photograph opposite). For the central carrot only, outline the right-hand side with pale orange.

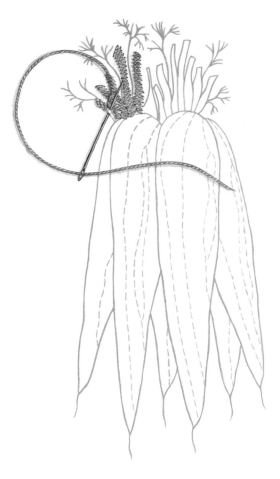

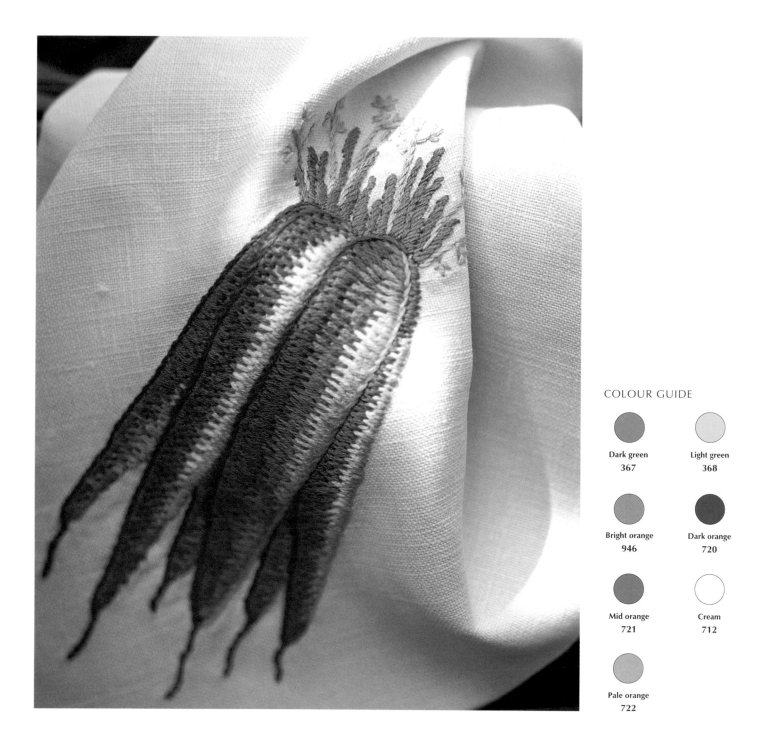

## COLOUR GUIDE

Dark green
367

Light green
368

Bright orange
946

Dark orange
720

Mid orange
721

Cream
712

Pale orange
722

# Geometrics and Initials

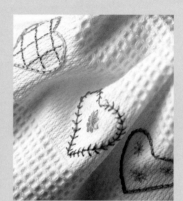

UNCOMPLICATED EMBROIDERY patterns are often the most effective and can turn an ordinary piece of household linen or length of fabric into something luxurious as well as personal. A curtain made from delicate lilac organza needs no more than a border of couched swirls to look magical, while a classic white napkin becomes exclusive when embroidered with an elegant initial. Geometric shapes and initials are also wonderfully versatile. They can be used singly, arranged in rows to form decorative bands (as in the Patterned Hearts project) or used at random over a large area. Different effects can be achieved by enlarging or reducing the scale of the motif, as well as by embroidering with different yarns. The blanket with the Sprinkled Snowflakes stitched in double knitting cotton is dramatically different from the coordinating sheet worked with fine thread, although similar templates were used. It would be exciting to use initials in this way, stitched at random over a blanket or bed cover. Sometimes it is the surface pattern or weave of a fabric that inspires a design. The checked fabric used for the Border of Crosses tablecloth and cushion lent itself beautifully to being filled with simple embroidery stitches arranged in geometric patterns. This treatment also adds textural interest to the surface of a fabric.

*LEFT: A diaphanous organza curtain is decoratively edged with cotton swirls made using couching stitch. The same pattern is reduced and applied to the contrasting tie-back. OPPOSITE: An elegant 'H' embroidered in satin stitch in a classic shade of navy blue adds a touch of luxury to a hand towel.*

# BORDER OF CROSSES

Both this tablecloth and cushion cover are ideal projects for the beginner, as the grid pattern of the fabric forms a guide in which to work the stitches. The crosses which form the building blocks for the two patterns are in fact double crosses, combining not only two different stitches, but also two different embroidery threads and colours. The first, and larger, diagonally formed cross is made up of four lazy daisy stitches, while the smaller straight cross sewn on top is formed from four straight stitches. Cream pearl cotton, a twisted thread with a sheen, alternates with stranded cotton in a contrasting colour. Alternating colours and threads in this way adds extra interest to an otherwise formal design.

*RIGHT: Checked fabrics offer endless possibilities for creating simple embroidery patterns. As with graph paper, the squares can be filled to form a shape or motif.*

## MATERIALS

- DMC Coton Perlé No. 5 in cream 712
- DMC stranded embroidery cotton in the following colours:
    maroon 3041 (*tablecloth only*)
    green 503 (*cushion cover only*)

For the size of tablecloth worked here allow approximately one skein of cream for three triangles and one skein of maroon for six triangles. For the cushion cover you will need two skeins each of cream and green.

*For the tablecloth*

- 2 x 1.5m (2⅛ x 1¾yd) of green and white checked cotton fabric with 2cm (¾in) squares (Fabric that is 142cm/56in wide will provide exactly the 71 squares width needed)

*For the cushion cover*

- 94 x 68cm (37 x 27in) of lilac and white checked cotton fabric with 2cm (¾in) squares
- 30cm (12in) zip
- 35cm (14in) thin foam pad

*For both projects*

- crewel (embroidery) needle size 5
- embroidery hoop

## STITCHES USED

lazy daisy stitch
straight stitch
For full details on stitches, see pages 132–7.

*ABOVE: The squares of a checked cushion cover are filled with lazy daisy and straight stitches to form a grid pattern.*

*LEFT: The same stitches are arranged on a tablecloth to create a border pattern of triangles, as well as textural interest.*

## TECHNIQUES

For full practical information on the methods used in this project, see pages 129–31.

### To work the tablecloth

First work out the arrangement of the pattern. Lay the fabric flat on the floor. Starting on a white square near one corner, count out a width of 67 squares and a length of 91 squares. Tuck under the remaining fabric while you count out the pattern. (Of this excess, two rows of squares all round are for hemming. Do not cut the excess yet, just in case you have made a mistake with the counting.) You should now have a white square on each corner.

Count along one width edge to the centre (the 34th square) and then count in four squares towards the centre. Mark this square with a pin. Count 12 squares to the left and mark the 12th square with

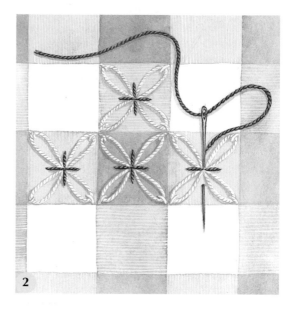

a second pin. The 11 squares between these two pins form the bottom line of the first triangle. The triangle narrows to one square over six rows (see photograph opposite) so count up five rows from the centre of the triangle base and mark the top of the triangle. Repeat to the left for the second triangle (leaving a dark square between each triangle) and then repeat twice on the right-hand side of the 34th square. You will now have four triangles marked out. Next mark the half triangles for the corners. These are six squares wide at their base.

Continue round the tablecloth, marking out six triangles on both lengths and four more on the other width, plus the corner triangles. The entire design is worked with six strands of thread. Start stitching at the top of each triangle, working four lazy daisy stitches in cream in a diagonal cross in each square (see 1 left). In the centre of each of these work four small straight stitches in maroon (see 2 above).

*1. In each square work four diagonally placed lazy daisy stitches. The small stitch holding down the loop of each lazy daisy stitch should point towards the corner of the square.*

*2. When the diagonal crosses are complete, work a smaller cross in a contrasting colour using four straight stitches. These are positioned evenly between the four lazy daisy stitches and should be of equal length.*

COLOUR GUIDE

**Cream**
**712**

**Green**
**503**

When all the triangles are complete, embroider the outer border line along the second row in from the edge (see photograph on page 73). Start in the centre of one edge. Work in the same stitches as for the triangles, but this time reverse the colours at each corner and at every sixth square. These reversed crosses should coincide with the middle of each triangle and the space between each triangle.

When the stitching is complete, hem the table-cloth with neat hand stitches, using the two rows of squares allowed for this. Cut off any excess fabric.

### To work the cushion cover

First work out the arrangement of the grid pattern. Lay the fabric flat on a table and, starting on a coloured square, count out a width of 17 squares and a height of 17 squares, leaving a margin of at least two rows of squares all round (one row for the seam and one for the decorative border). You should have a coloured square in each corner. The embroidery is worked along this outer line of squares and every fourth row, thus forming a grid pattern. Work the stitches within each square as for the tablecloth. Reverse the colours every fourth square, where the grid lines cross (see photograph opposite).

### To make up the cushion cover

Cut round the embroidery, including the border of two squares all round. For the backing fabric mark out two pieces of matching fabric, one piece measuring 42 x 12cm (16½ x 4¾in), or 21 squares by six squares, and the other piece 42 x 34cm (16½ x 13½in), or 21 squares by 17 squares. Place the two pieces right sides together and, using a sewing machine or small back stitches, join along one long edge, using one row of squares as the seam allowance and leaving enough seam open in the middle for the length of the zip. Press the seam flat. Pin, tack and then stitch the zip into position.

With right sides facing and the zip open, pin, tack and machine stitch the embroidery to the backing fabric, leaving one row of squares all round as your seam allowance. Snip across the corners to avoid a bulky finish and turn the cushion cover to the right side. Press the seam well. Machine stitch all around the outside edge of the border of squares (see photograph opposite). Insert the cushion.

Cut out four cushion ties from the fabric remains, each 45 x 4cm (18 x 1½in). Fold each strip in half lengthways, right sides together, and machine stitch along the long side and one short end. With the blunt end of a pencil, turn each tube right side out. Press. Tuck in the open end and hand stitch to close. Position the ties in pairs on the underneath of the cushion so they can be tied round the back of the chair, and hand sew in place.

### Using checked fabrics

There are many different checked fabrics available, from tiny gingham checks to bold grids. Woven checks are more suitable for embroidery, printed check fabrics usually being too flimsy. If you can't find the same sized check as the one used here, you can use a smaller check, although the resulting pattern will be smaller. To obtain the same scale of design, work more squares for each triangle. For a different effect altogether use a small check and embroider each cross over several squares.

# SIMPLE SWIRLS

This straightforward loop design, like an orderly and neatly repeating scribble or doodle, is ideally suited to couching. With couching stitch, the only stitch used for this design, the main embroidery thread is laid across the surface of the fabric, and held in place with another – often contrasting – thread. This allows for enormous scope in mixing different threads and fabrics together as well as working bold designs. I have been able to use a thick knitting cotton with a fragile organza because, unlike the other embroidery stitches in this book, the nature of couching stitch means that the main thread does not pass in and out of the fabric.

*LEFT AND OPPOSITE: Swirls and loops add decorative detail to the edge of an exquisite organza curtain as well as embellishing a tie-back made in contrasting fabric.*

## MATERIALS

- 1 x 50gm (1¾oz) ball of double knitting cotton
- DMC stranded embroidery cotton in the following colours:
    cream 712 (*curtain only*)
    lilac 554 (*tie-back only*)
    For the curtain border, allow one skein of cream for approximately 120cm (48in) of embroidery. For the tie-back, one skein of each colour is plenty.
- ready-made curtains or, if you wish to make your own, organza or any other sheer fabric made up as required
- 76 x 40cm (30 x 16in) of loose-woven cream cotton or linen fabric for the tie-back
- masking tape
- water-soluble pen
- crewel (embroidery) needle size 6
- dressmaker's carbon paper

## STITCHES USED

couching stitch

For full details on stitches, see pages 132–7.

## TECHNIQUES

For full practical information on the methods used in this project, see pages 129–31.

### To work the curtain border

Enlarge the template on page 79 to 280% on a photocopier. Place the copy on a flat surface such as a table and secure in position with masking tape.

Continue tracing the pattern, moving the fabric over the copy until the repeating pattern runs down the whole length of the curtain.

Start stitching, working from right to left. Bring the double knitting cotton up through the fabric at the right-hand end of the swirl line. Following the line of the pattern, hold the thread down with small vertical stitches of embroidery cotton (see 1 left). Inside each large loop work one small loose loop, held in place at its base with one or two stitches (see 2 below).

**To work the curtain tie-back**

Mark out two strips of fabric 66 x 11cm (26 x 4½in). Add a 2cm (¾in) seam allowance all round and cut out. Put one piece aside for the backing. On the tie-back front mark three lines down the length of the fabric with the water-soluble pen, one line in the centre and the other two on either side, 2.5cm (1in) from the edge (including the seam allowance). Enlarge the template opposite to 130% and transfer it onto the tie-back using dressmaker's

*1. With the thread to be couched laid along the pattern line, make small, evenly spaced stitches to hold it in position. As you stitch, the couched thread should lie smoothly on the surface of the fabric, and should not be too slack or pulled so tight that it wrinkles the material.*

*2. When one large loop has been completed, make another, smaller loop over it. With just one or two vertical stitches, secure in place at the point where the yarn crosses both loops. The rest of the small loop is left unstitched so that it falls freely away from the fabric when the curtain is hung.*

Place the curtain over this, starting at the bottom of the leading (or inside) edge if the border is intended for the right side of a window, or at the top of the leading (or inside) edge for a curtain on the left side of the window. You will be able to see the pattern through the fabric. Position the fabric so that the pattern is level with the edge and secure to the table for a moment with tape. With a water-soluble pen, lightly trace the pattern directly onto the fabric.

carbon paper, keeping the pattern level between the lines and reversing it on one side for a mirror effect (see photograph right). Work couching stitch along all the lines as for the curtain border, but use lilac embroidery cotton for the holding stitches and omit the small loose loop.

**To make up the tie-back**

With right sides facing, place the embroidered strip over the backing. Machine stitch along the two long sides and one short end. Snip the corners diagonally to get rid of excess fabric before turning the tube to the right side. Press. Tuck in the open end and hand stitch closed.

To make the ties for the tie-back cut two strips of fabric, each 45 x 4cm (18 x 1½in). Fold each strip in half lengthways, right sides together. Machine stitch along the long side and one short end. With the blunt end of a pencil, turn each tube right side out. Press. Tuck in each open end and hand stitch to close. Hand sew the ties onto the tie-back, one at each end in the centre.

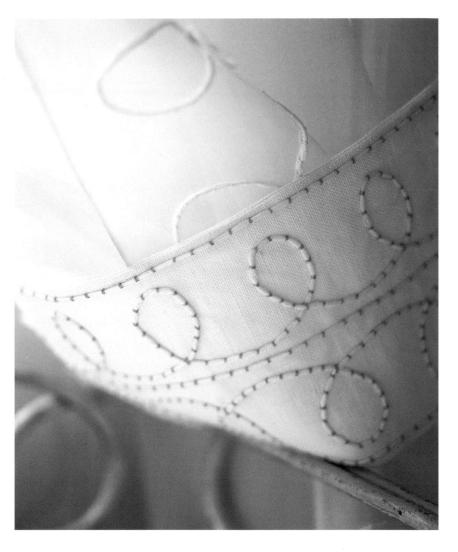

TEMPLATE

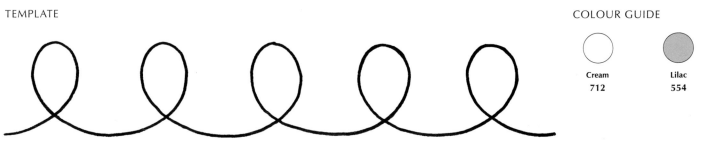

COLOUR GUIDE

Cream
712

Lilac
554

# PATTERNED HEARTS

The heart is one of the most extensively used motifs in folk art. It has been painted on dowry chests, embroidered on cloth and carved into furniture and over doors. Its symbolism embraces friendship, loyalty and warmth, as well as love.

    The heart designs shown here, although traditional in their use and arrangement, look modern and fresh. This is largely due to the choice of colours. There is no trace of the familiar red; instead, the colours are reminiscent of spring flowers, daffodils and lilac. While small shapes such as petals and leaves are ideally suited to solid stitching, larger-scale motifs, such as these hearts, look best filled with relatively open stitches or simple patterns.

*RIGHT: Basic stitches and shapes in the prettiest of colours are combined in a decorative band across a honeycomb-weave towel. The pattern can be fully appreciated when the towel is draped over a rail or basin.*

## MATERIALS

- DMC stranded embroidery cotton in the following colours:
    - yellow 3821
    - lilac 340
    - green 913
    - pink 3806
    - purple 554 (*except single-motif hand towel*)

One skein of each colour is more than sufficient to work the embroidered shelving cloth with 14 hearts, as well as a repeat-motif and a single-motif hand towel.

- plain white cotton or linen fabric for shelving cloth (see page 82 to calculate quantity)
- length of lace trimming to fit shelving cloth
- cotton hand towels
- tracing paper
- crewel (embroidery) needle size 6
- dressmaker's carbon paper
- embroidery hoop

## STITCHES USED

| | |
|---|---|
| chain stitch | back stitch |
| straight stitch | fern stitch |
| lazy daisy stitch | |

For full details on stitches, see pages 132–7.

## TECHNIQUES

For full practical information on the methods used in this project, refer to Techniques on pages 129–31.

*ABOVE: The pattern used for the shelving cloth is equally effective on a hand towel. For the second hand towel, two hearts have been combined to form a different design. LEFT: A glimpse inside a half-open cupboard reveals carefully stacked shelves covered with a cloth edged with lace and embroidered hearts.*

**1**

**2**

*1. For each star make eight straight stitches from the centre of each dot, as marked on the template. To ensure that the stitches radiate symmetrically, work a cross first, then the diagonal stitches.*

*2. The outline of the fern stitch heart is worked in two halves, each starting with a back stitch.*

**To work the shelving cloth**

Measure the length and width of the shelf, adding 6cm (2½in) to the width for the embroidered border and a further 2.5cm (1in) all round for the hem allowance. Mark these measurements on the cotton or linen fabric and cut out.

Trace the three different templates opposite. Using a tape measure and sewing pins, plan the placement of the hearts. I positioned mine 7.5cm (3in) apart (measuring from the centre of one heart to the next) and 4cm (1½in) from the bottom (including the hem allowance). Using dressmaker's carbon paper, transfer the hearts onto the fabric (see photograph on page 81 for order).

The entire design is worked with three strands of thread. Work the three different hearts as follows.

### GRID HEART

The heart with the grid pattern is outlined in chain stitch in yellow. Start at the top and work round one side to the point. Repeat on the other side. Embroider the grid in lilac using back stitch.

### THREE-STAR HEART

The heart with three stars is also outlined in chain stitch, but this time in lilac. The yellow stars are made from eight straight stitches radiating out from a central point; this is known as Algerian Eye stitch. Bring the thread through the centre of the marked dot and make one straight stitch horizontally to the left. Bring the needle up in the centre again and make a second stitch, this time vertically (see 1 above). Work two more straight stitches in this way to form a cross, before working four diagonal stitches in between. Try to keep the stitches symmetrical.

### FERN STITCH HEART

The third heart, worked in two colourways, is outlined with pink or green fern stitch. Starting at the top, work one back stitch, before continuing in fern stitch round one side to the point. Repeat for the other side (see 2 above). For the star in the middle of the heart, embroider eight green or purple radiating lazy daisy stitches, all emerging from one central point.

## To make up the shelving cloth

When you have finished the embroidery, hem the shelving cloth all round and add the lace trimming.

## To work the repeat-motif hand towel

This is worked in exactly the same way and to the same scale as the shelving cloth above.

## To work the single-motif hand towel

For the outer heart, enlarge the central template below to 200% on a photocopier. For the inner heart, simply trace the same template. Using dressmaker's carbon paper, transfer the hearts onto the corner of the towel. I placed mine 5cm (2in) from the side and 7.5cm (3in) from the bottom. Ensure that the smaller heart is centrally placed inside the larger heart.

The entire design is worked with three strands of thread, except for the outline of the larger heart which is worked with six strands. Work both outlines in chain stitch, using pink for the large heart and lilac for the smaller one. Between the two outlines embroider nine yellow stars in straight stitch, and in the centre work one green star in lazy daisy stitch, as for the shelving cloth.

TEMPLATES

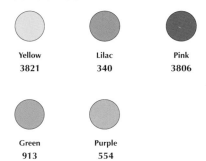

COLOUR GUIDE

| Yellow 3821 | Lilac 340 | Pink 3806 |
| Green 913 | Purple 554 | |

# ELEGANT INITIALS

During the nineteenth century it became extremely fashionable to embellish all your possessions with your initials, from crystal, china and silverware to luggage. Even household linen did not escape the trend. Each piece was embroidered with letters taken from alphabets in a multitude of different styles, from the plain and unadorned to the very complex. Some letters were used purely for identification purposes, to enable laundry staff to distinguish one batch of white linen from another. Others were lavishly entwined to form highly decorative monograms, and were used as embellishments, for example, in the centre of grand formal tablecloths. Inspired by this tradition, the letters illustrated here will allow you to add a touch of elegance to your own household linen.

## MATERIALS

- DMC stranded embroidery cotton in the following colours:
     navy 336 (*hand towel only*)
     blue 798 (*napkins only*)
  One skein is sufficient to embroider four napkins or three hand towels.
- plain cotton or linen hand towel
- plain cotton or linen napkins or, if you prefer to make your own, plain cotton or linen fabric. Allow a 50cm (20in) square of fabric for each napkin.
- crewel (embroidery) needle size 5 or 6
- dressmaker's carbon paper
- embroidery hoop

*LEFT: A set of beautiful linen napkins is personalized with elegant letters embroidered in royal blue thread.*
*OPPOSITE: A single letter 'H', taken from the same alphabet on page 88 but greatly enlarged, gives an old hand towel a new lease of life.*

*RIGHT: When the outline shape of the letter narrows down to a single thin line, replace satin stitch with small back stitches. As soon as the line begins to thicken, return to working in satin stitch.*

## STITCHES USED

satin stitch

back stitch

For full details on stitches, see pages 132–7.

## TECHNIQUES

For full practical information on methods used in this project, see pages 129–31. Although for many embroidery projects I think hoops are optional, they are essential for initials and monograms, where the success of the work is dependent upon the smoothness and the closeness of the satin stitches.

### To work the hand towel

Enlarge the initial of your choice from pages 88 and 89 to 245% on a photocopier. Using dressmaker's carbon paper, transfer the initial onto the towel, placing it near the bottom where it will be visible when hung over a towel rail. Mount the fabric in the embroidery hoop.

The entire design is worked with three strands of thread and in satin stitch only. This is one of the most popular stitches used for embroidering letters. Work the stitches from side to side to create a solid band of colour (see the cross-stroke of the 'A' in illustration left). As the lines of the letters curl, turn the angle of the needle so that the stitches continue to lie at 90 degrees to the strokes of the letter. The stitches must not slant between these lines. Make sure that no fabric shows through between each stitch, and that all stitches lie perfectly flat on the fabric.

### To work the napkins

Enlarge the initial of your choice to 140% on a photocopier. Using dressmaker's carbon paper, transfer the initial onto the corner of the napkin. (Be careful not to place the initial too close to the corner or you will not be able to mount the napkin in the hoop.)

The entire design is worked with three strands of thread. Stitch most of the letter in satin stitch, working from side to side of the outline, but where the strokes of the letter are reduced to a fine line, work in very small back stitch (see illustration left). Make sure no fabric is visible between each stitch.

COLOUR GUIDE

**Blue
798**

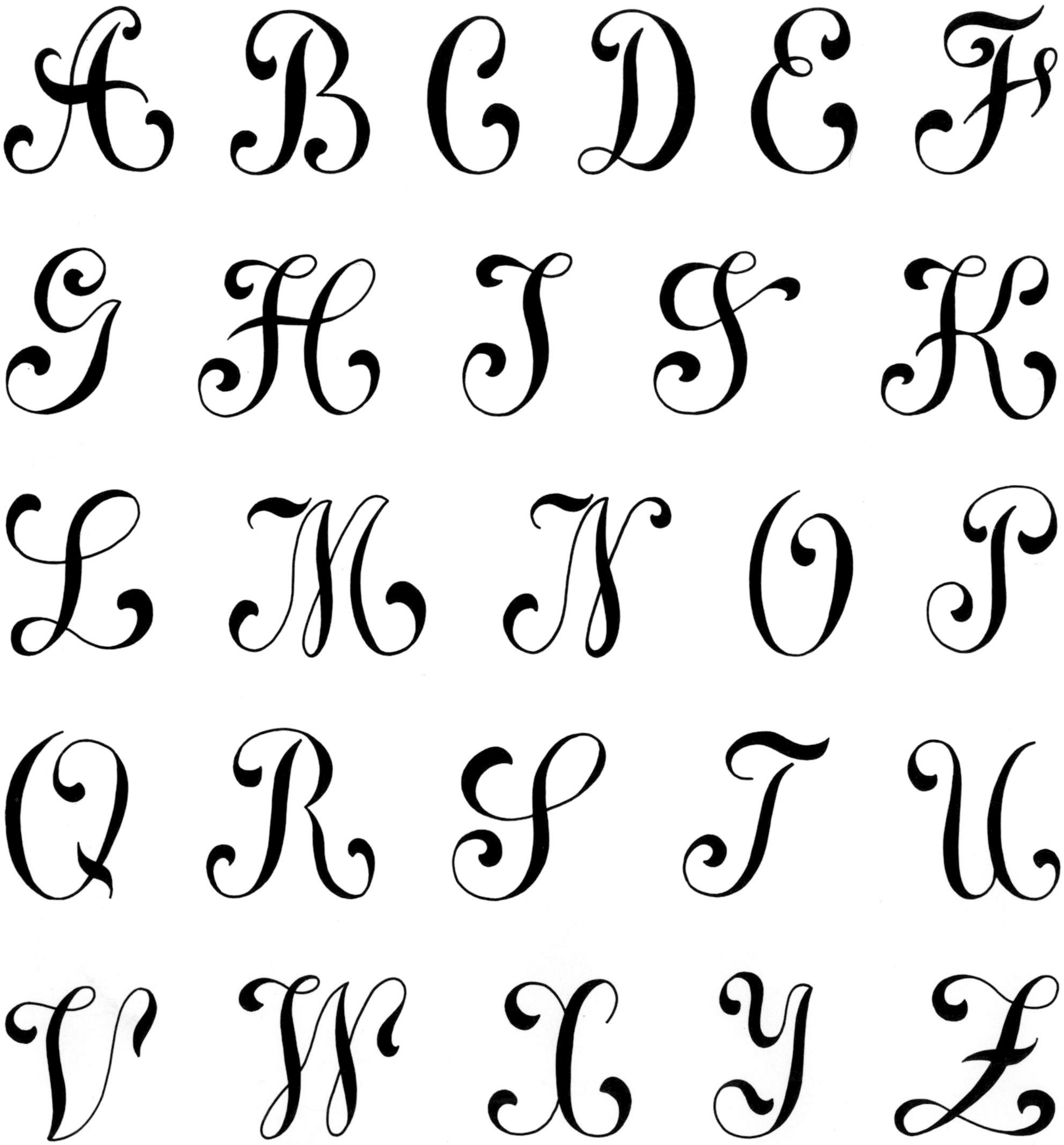

A B C D E F
G H I J K
L M N O P
Q R S T U
V W X Y Z

A B C D E F
G H I J K L M
N O P Q R S T
U V W X Y Z

# SPRINKLED SNOWFLAKES

This snowflake project is a good illustration of how the scale of an image, and the type of embroidery thread and fabric, can completely alter a design. For the main project, two different snowflakes are repeated in an orderly row along the edge of a smooth cotton sheet and daintily worked in silky yarn using three different embroidery stitches. For the variation on the theme, a third snowflake template is dramatically enlarged and randomly scattered over a fluffy wool blanket. To complement the texture of the blanket, the snowflakes are stitched robustly in satin stitch, using cream double knitting cotton and a darning needle.

*RIGHT AND OPPOSITE:*
*A sprinkling of snowflakes*
*enhances a plain cotton*
*sheet and a wool blanket.*
*The different scale and*
*arrangements of snowflakes*
*in the two designs are further*
*emphasized by the sharply*
*contrasting embroidery threads.*

## MATERIALS

- DMC stranded embroidery cotton in the following colour:
  yellow 726
  Quantities used depend on the size of sheet. For a single sheet, two skeins are sufficient.
- plain cotton or linen sheet or, if you prefer to make your own, cotton sheeting or linen
- tracing paper
- crewel (embroidery) needle size 6
- dressmaker's carbon paper
- embroidery hoop

## STITCHES USED

lazy daisy stitch
back stitch
fly stitch
For full details on stitches used, see pages 132–7.

## TECHNIQUES

For full practical information on methods used in this project, see pages 129–31.

### To work the sheet border

Photocopy the left- and right-hand templates on page 92, taking plenty of copies. Using a tape measure and sewing pins, plan their placement. I placed my larger snowflakes 20cm (8in) apart (measuring from the centre of one to the other) and 4cm (1½in) from the edge of the sheet. In between these, I evenly positioned three small snowflakes. Using dressmaker's carbon paper, transfer the pattern onto the sheet.

TEMPLATES

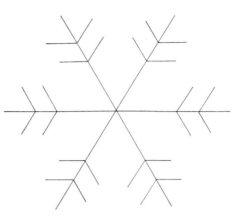

COLOUR GUIDE

Yellow
726

The entire design is worked with three strands of thread. For the larger of the two snowflakes, start at one end of one of the long radiating lines. Work the tip and the four short strokes in lazy daisy stitch. Continue down the line in back stitch to the other end, and then repeat the five lazy daisy stitches. Repeat for the other two lines to complete the snowflake (see photograph left).

For the smaller snowflake, simply work each radiating line in fly stitch (see 1 below). Traditionally, the loop of fly stitch is secured with a small vertical stitch, but here the stitch extends to the centre of the snowflake (see 2 below). Repeat both large and small snowflakes as often as required.

*1. For each radiating line of the smaller snowflake, pick up a diagonal stitch, with the needle point over the loop.*
*2. To hold the loop in place, make a vertical stitch that extends to the centre of the snowflake. Bring the needle out where the next diagonal stitch is to be worked.*

**1**

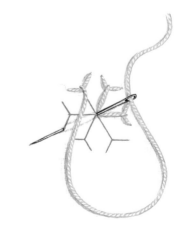

**2**

## To work the design on a blanket

For a coordinating blanket, you will need to stencil the motif in place rather than use dressmaker's carbon paper, because of the fluffy nature of blanket fleece. On a photocopier, enlarge the larger snowflake template (right) to 230% and the smaller one (centre, page 92) to 220%. Make several copies for planning the placement. Paste one copy of each snowflake shape onto separate pieces of thin card, making sure there is plenty of excess card around the motifs. With a craft knife, carefully cut out the snowflakes to leave two stencils.

Plan the placement of the snowflakes using the extra photocopies of the motifs, then pin them temporarily in place. Lay the blanket on a smooth, flat surface and place the correct stencil in the required position. Spray the stencil very lightly with spray paint in order just to mark the snowflake on the blanket with a fine mist. Very carefully remove the stencil and allow the paint to dry thoroughly. Repeat for the required number of snowflakes.

Using a darning needle and a 50g (1¾oz) ball of double knitting cotton in cream, embroider the snowflakes in satin stitch (see photographs below and overleaf for direction of stitches).

TEMPLATE

# FLORAL MONOGRAMS

The stitches that look simplest are not always the easiest to work. Satin stitch is a good example of this: to work one stitch is easy, but to work stitches in a group requires care and precision. The outer edges of a shape filled with satin stitch should be even, with each stitch lying satin-smooth over the fabric and in line with the next stitch. As a general guide, the simpler the working method of a stitch, the more practice is required for a perfect finish.

While the Elegant Initials (see page 84) show how effective satin stitch can be, these Floral Monograms are also raised with padding stitches. The light catches the curve of each raised stitch and intensifies the sheen and colour of the thread.

*ABOVE AND RIGHT:*
*The prettiest way to*
*personalize a linen pillowcase*
*or a folder is to frame your*
*monogram with a garland*
*of leaves and flowers.*

## MATERIALS
- DMC stranded embroidery cotton in the following colours:
    lilac 211 (*pillowcase only*)
    cream 712 (*folder only*)
  Allow four skeins for the pillowcase and three for the folder, although these quantities will vary depending on the amount of padding you do.

*For the pillowcase*
- cotton or linen pillowcase or, if you prefer to make your own, 1m (1¼yd) of cotton sheeting or linen

*For the folder*
- 50cm (20in) of coloured cotton or linen
- two pieces of 2mm (¹⁄₁₆in) thick card, 35 x 25cm (14 x 10in)
- one piece of thinner card or heavy paper large enough to line the folder
- strong glue
- masking tape

*For both projects*
- crewel (embroidery) needle size 5
- dressmaker's carbon paper
- embroidery hoop

## STITCHES USED
padded satin stitch
stem stitch
For full details on stitches used, see pages 132–7.

## TECHNIQUES

For full practical information on methods used in this project, see pages 129–31.

### To work the pillowcase

On a photocopier, enlarge the floral template below to 300% and the initials of your choice from pages 88 and 89 to 235%. With a pin or a couple of tacking stitches, mark the centre of the pillowcase. Using dressmaker's carbon paper, first transfer the flowers, placing the cross over the tacking stitches to give you the correct position. Into the centre of this floral frame place the initials, so that the bottom of each letter is level with the tacking stitches. Make sure both the flowers and the letters are level with the outline of the pillowcase.

The entire design is worked with three strands of thread. First pad the flowers, leaves and letters. Work rows of small running stitches to fill the outline of each shape (see illustration above). The closer together the stitches, the more raised each shape

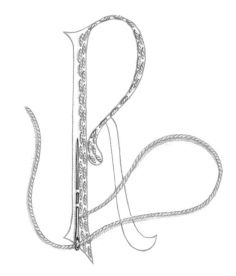

will be. Work satin stitch over this padding, referring to the template for the direction of the stitches. Work a single row of stem stitch to follow each stem line.

### To work the folder

Cut two pieces of fabric (one for the front of the folder and the other for the back) 41cm (16in) wide by 31cm (12in) high. On a photocopier, enlarge the floral template (left) to 240% and the initials of your choice from pages 88 and 89 to 185%. To em–broider the front, work exactly as for the pillowcase.

### To make up the folder

Press the two fabric pieces. Sew them together along one side edge. Press, then join the two pieces of 2mm (¹⁄₁₆in) thick card along one side edge with masking tape, taping on both sides to form a spine. Position the hinged cardboard piece open over the back of the embroidery and the backing fabric, so that the spine aligns with the seam. Cut the fabric

TEMPLATE

corners diagonally. Fold the overlaps, 2.5cm (1in) all round, over the card to the inside and tape or glue in place. Position the thinner card or paper for the inside of the folder over the back of the hinged card to cover the fabric overlaps. Glue in place. Place under a heavy object to dry for at least an hour. On the inside of the folder score down the centre of the lining card or paper to make a spine. Fold in half.

# Home and Hearth

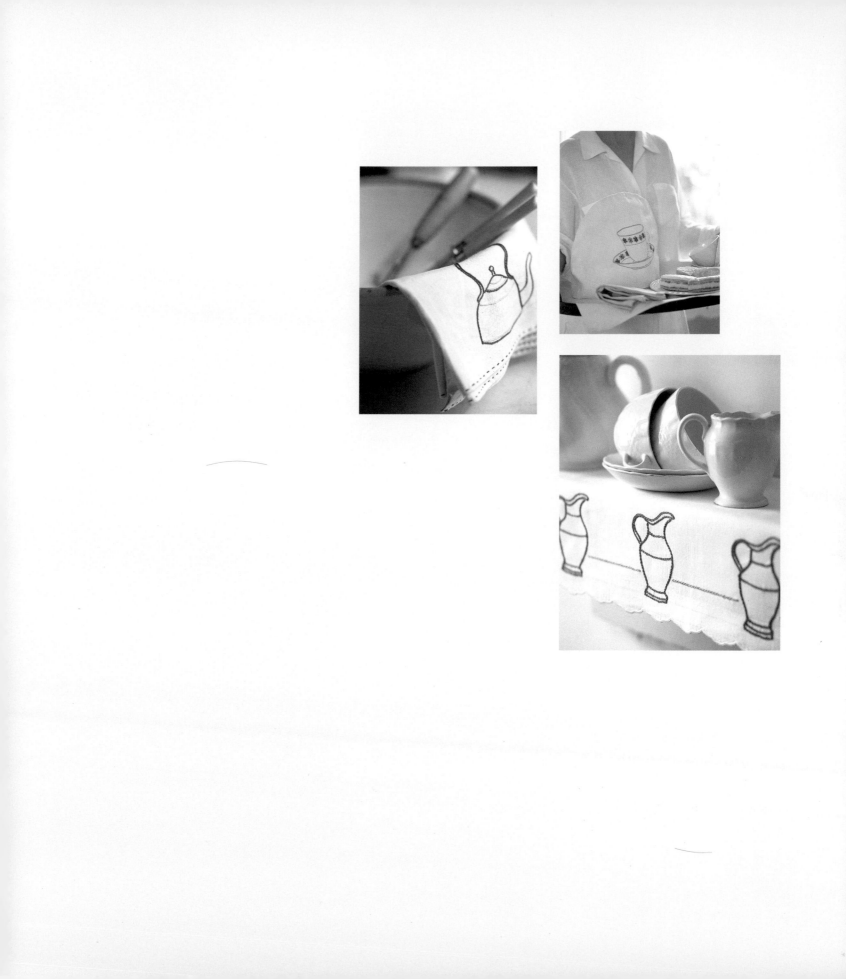

FLOWERS, ANIMALS, BIRDS and simple geometric patterns are the subjects we most associate with embroidery. Equally effective, though little used, are images taken from the home. An elegant water jug, a glass perfume bottle, an old-fashioned iron and a curvaceous wrought-iron chair are all examples of interesting shapes that can be interpreted successfully in embroidery. Because household utensils and furniture are such strong motifs, I chose to keep the embroidery at its simplest, often using stitches such as chain or stem to outline the shape, and limiting myself to just one or two colours. This gives the motif the appearance of a line drawing. I find the resulting simplicity of the patterns very attractive. Different effects could be achieved by introducing more colours and stitches. Within the outline stitches, areas could be filled with lines of chain stitch, placed close together, for textural interest; or long and short stitch could be used to shade the side of a motif.

Where possible I have put the finished embroideries to practical use, or at least used them in the rooms from which the designs were gathered. Hence a shelving cloth decorated with a row of kettles and mugs looks wonderful on a kitchen dresser, and a teacup is perfectly placed on a tea-cosy for afternoon tea.

*LEFT: The elegant curves of a wrought-iron chair find an echo in the miniature curlicue chairs embroidered onto a cushion cover.*

*OPPOSITE: An old-fashioned water jug and bowl in shades of blue and lilac are embroidered onto a piece of white fabric, which in turn is sewn onto a checked wash basin skirt. Rather than overpowering the embroidery, the contrasting fabrics act as an effective frame.*

# KITCHEN WARES

The simplicity and naivety of the embroidered kitchen utensils is what makes these shelf borders and glass cloth so appealing. The fun of designing them lies in choosing the objects to be embroidered. Almost any kitchen utensil, as long as it has an interesting shape, can be represented with embroidery. For the shelf borders, you could add other motifs to work alongside those shown here to tell a story. Or, for a completely different effect, but one that is equally striking, you could arrange the utensils informally over a tablecloth, as for the Scattered Leaves project (see page 22), and make matching napkins embroidered with one or more motifs.

ABOVE: Kitchen shelves lined with lengths of cotton fabric embroidered with water jugs, kettles and mugs.
RIGHT: An old-fashioned iron adorns the corner of a glass cloth.

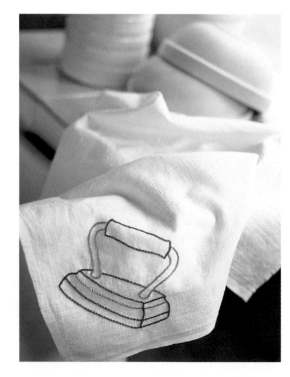

## MATERIALS

- DMC stranded embroidery cotton in the following colours:
  - orange 350
  - yellow 3821
  - mid blue 798
  - pale blue 799

Each of my shelving cloths is 112cm (44in) long and embroidered with nine utensils. To work these, two skeins of the main colours (orange and mid blue) and one of the contrasting colours would be sufficient. For one large motif on a glass cloth, one skein of each colour is plenty.

- plain white cotton or linen fabric, or old sheeting with scalloped edges for the shelving cloth
- ready-made cotton or linen glass cloth or, if you prefer to make your own, sufficient cotton or linen fabric
- crewel (embroidery) needle size 6
- dressmaker's carbon paper
- embroidery hoop

## STITCHES USED

stem stitch (*kettle, mug and iron*)
chain stitch (*water jug*)
running stitch (*shelf border*)
For full details on stitches used, see pages 132–7.

## TECHNIQUES

For full practical information on methods used in this project, see pages 129–31.

*LEFT: In addition to outlining designs with strong colours, choosing a single image and working it in a repeat pattern also helps to emphasize the clean shapes of kitchen utensils.*

## To work the kettle and mug border

Measure out a strip of fabric to the length and width of your shelf, adding 12.5cm (5in) to the width for the embroidered border and a further 2.5cm (1in) all round for the hem allowance. Cut out.

Enlarge the kettle and mug templates below to 160% on a photocopier. Using a tape measure and sewing pins, plan the placement of the utensils, alternating the kettle and mug. To help position the motifs so that their bases are all level, tack a line of running stitches in contrasting thread 5cm (2in) from the bottom edge of the fabric. Transfer the motifs onto the border with dressmaker's carbon paper, using the stitched line for placement.

The entire design is worked in stem stitch with three strands of thread. The outline of the kettle and the base of its lid are in orange and the decorative banding in yellow. The mug has a yellow outline and an orange stripe.

When the embroidery is complete, remove any tacking stitches. Hand sew a 2.5cm (1in) hem all round. Work a row of running stitches in orange along the bottom edge using three threads.

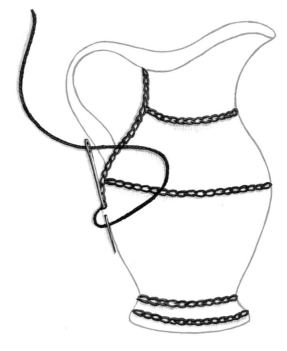

## To work the water jug border

If you do not have a piece of fabric or old sheeting with a scalloped edging, work with a straight edge as for the previous border. Enlarge the jug template above to 185% on a photocopier. Use three strands

TEMPLATES

of thread, as for the kettle and mug border, but embroider in chain stitch rather than stem stitch using either orange or mid blue for the outline and banding (refer to the caption on page 106 for the order of work). When the jugs are complete, work a line of chain stitch in either yellow or pale blue between each motif.

**To work the glass cloth**

Enlarge the utensil of your choice (I have used an iron, for which the template is provided below) to 180% on a photocopier. Using dressmaker's carbon paper, transfer the design onto the cloth, placing it across one of the corners (see photograph on page 104) where it will be visible when hung over a rack. Be careful not to place the motif too near the cloth edge, or you will not be able to mount the fabric into the hoop. The entire design is worked in stem stitch with four strands of thread (refer to the photograph for the use of colour).

First work the iron base, starting with the three horizontal lines and then the outline. Next work the sides of the handle before completing the top part.

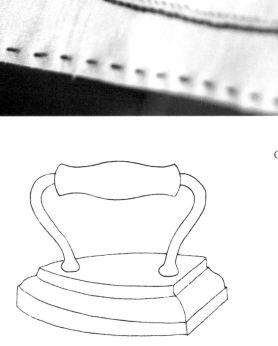

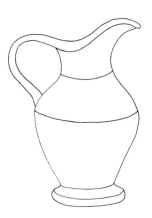

COLOUR GUIDE

Orange
350

Yellow
3821

# CURLICUE CHAIRS

This project was inspired by the elegant forms of wrought-iron chairs, with their elaborate curls, lattice seats and numerous variations in style. The chair frames on the cushion cover are embroidered in couching stitch using double knitting cotton, rather than fine embroidery cotton, as the surface thread. The thickness of yarn gives a raised, almost three-dimensional effect, which successfully replicates the roundness of the wrought-iron tubing.

In contrast, the chairs on the curtain tie-back are worked in chain stitch, which results in the embroidery having a flatter appearance. Both the tie-back and the cushion are fringed, which gives an element of fun as well as textural interest.

*BELOW: A row of chairs stitched in chain stitch with cream thread decorates a pale green tie-back. OPPOSITE: The chairs look equally elegant on a pale blue cushion, placed on a wrought-iron chair that mirrors the designs.*

## MATERIALS
- DMC stranded embroidery cotton in the following colour:
    cream 712
    For the cushion cover allow one skein and for the tie-back two skeins.

*For the cushion cover*
- 1 x 50gm (1¾oz) ball of double knitting cotton
- 1m x 50cm (40 x 20in) of coloured linen or cotton fabric. This should be of sufficiently loose weave to allow the double knitting cotton to pass through easily without distorting the fabric.
- 35cm (14in) zip
- 40cm (16in) cushion pad
- 2m (2⅛yd) of fringing

*For the tie-back*
- 25cm (10in) of coloured linen or cotton
- 1.5m (1¾yd) of fringing
- 50cm (20in) of 2.5cm (1in) wide cotton tape for ties

*For both projects*
- set square
- crewel (embroidery) needle size 6
- dressmaker's carbon paper
- embroidery hoop

## STITCHES USED
French knot
back stitch
couching stitch (*cushion cover only*)
chain stitch (*tie-back only*)
For full details on stitches, see pages 132–7.

## TECHNIQUES
For full practical information on the methods used in this project, see pages 129–31.

### To work the cushion cover
Using a set square and a ruler, mark out a rectangle 42 x 40cm (16½ x 16in). Add a 2.5cm (1in) seam allowance all round and cut out. Enlarge each of the three chair motifs on pages 112 and 113 twice to 190% on a photocopier. Using dressmaker's carbon paper, transfer the chairs onto the fabric, arranging them in two rows 5cm (2in) apart vertically, measuring from the base of the chairs in the top row to the

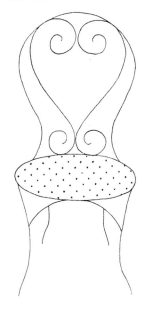

top of the chairs in the lower row, and 13cm (5in) apart horizontally, measuring from the centre of one chair to the next.

Work the chair seats first. For the chair motif with the dotted seat, work one French knot for each dot using six strands of thread. For the chair with the lattice seat and back, work the grid pattern in back stitch using four strands of thread. For the third style of chair, work the lattice seat also in back stitch but with six strands of thread (see 1 below).

Work the rest of each chair in couching stitch. Bring the double knitting cotton up through the fabric at the beginning of a swirl, a line or a shape. Following the line of the pattern, hold the thread down with small vertical stitches using three strands of embroidery cotton. For a very curved shape, for example the swirls on the chair backs, the stitches should be worked closer than for those along a straighter line to create smoother lines (see 2 below).

At the end of each line, take both the threads back to the wrong side. For circular shapes, this will also be the starting point.

**To make up the cushion cover**

For the backing fabric you will need to mark out two pieces of fabric, one piece measuring 40 x 10cm (16 x 4in) and the other 40 x 32cm (16 x 12¼in). Add a 2.5cm (1in) seam allowance all round and cut out. Place the two pieces right sides together, and, using a sewing machine or small back stitches, join along one long edge, leaving enough seam open in the middle for the length of the zip. Press the seams flat. Pin, tack and then stitch the zip into position. With right sides facing and the zip open, pin and tack the backing fabric to the embroidery, placing the fringing between the two layers. Machine sew all round, leaving a 2.5cm (1in) seam allowance. Snip across the corners and turn the

*1. Work the grid pattern of each chair seat in back stitch. The needle is brought up and down only at the points where the grid lines cross.*

*2. To achieve a good curl, the couched thread should be stitched down more frequently along the curves of the design than along the straight lines.*

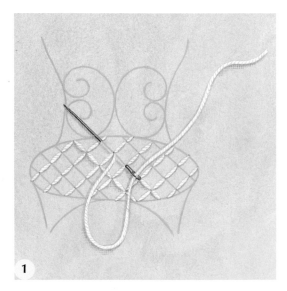

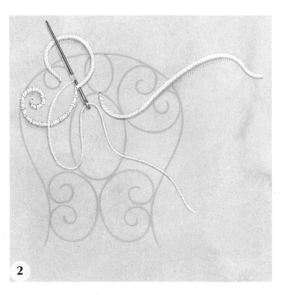

cushion cover right side out. Press. Trim the fringing down to the required length, if necessary.

**To work the curtain tie-back**

Mark out two strips of fabric 57 x 13cm (22½ x 5in). Add a 2.5cm (1in) seam allowance all round and cut out. Put one piece aside for the backing.

Enlarge the chair templates on page 112 and below to 135% on a photocopier. You will need eight chairs. Place these in a line along the length of the fabric 7.5cm (3in) apart, measuring from the centre of one chair to the next. The base line should measure 4cm (1½in) from the fabric edge, including the seam allowance.

All the chairs are worked with four strands of embroidery thread. Start stitching, working the chair seats first as given above for the cushion cover. Complete the chairs in chain stitch rather than couching stitch, and work a short row of six or seven chain stitches in between each chair and a line of chain stitch just under the chairs.

**To make up the tie-back**

With right sides facing, pin and tack the embroidery to the backing, placing the fringing between the two layers, pointing inwards. Machine stitch along the two long sides and one short end. Snip the corners diagonally to get rid of excess fabric, then turn to right side. Press. Tuck in the open end and stitch closed.

To make the ties, cut the tape into two equal pieces and fold each strip in half lengthwise, tucking in the ends. Machine stitch all round, as near to the edge as possible. Hand sew the ties onto the tie-back, one at each end in the centre.

COLOUR GUIDE

Cream
**712**

TEMPLATES

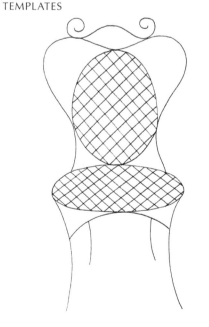

# BATHTIME

*Although there are many similarities between this project and Kitchen Wares (see page 104) – for example, the simple outlining of objects, the choice of stitches and restrained colour schemes – the approach to the layout and the application of the designs onto fabric is quite different. These motifs are not applied directly onto the checked fabric but first embroidered onto small pieces of white fabric. These are then cut and sewn onto the wash basin skirt or bag, much as you would sew patchwork pieces onto a quilt. The lilac running stitch that holds the pieces in place frames each image. For the basin skirt the designs are arranged in a loose, informal way, with no trace of a repeating pattern.*

**MATERIALS**

- DMC stranded embroidery cotton in the following colours:
     pale blue 809
     lilac 340
     mid blue 3807
  For the draw-string bag, one skein of each colour is plenty. For the wash basin skirt, quantities will depend on the number of patchwork pieces embroidered. I used eight motifs on mine, for which two skeins each of mid blue and lilac and one skein of pale blue sufficed.

*For the wash basin skirt*

- checked fabric measuring one-and-a-half times the width of the basin (or area to be covered) by the distance from the basin to the floor. Add a 7.5cm (3in) hem and heading allowance to the length and 5cm (2in) to the width for side hems.
- hanging wire from which to suspend the skirt, to the width of the basin (or area to be covered)

*For the draw-string bag*

- 80 x 70cm (31½ x 27½in) of checked fabric
- 76cm (30in) of cord

*For both projects*

- white cotton sheeting, enough to create as many patchwork pieces as required. To achieve a satisfactory result the fabric should be of the same weight and thickness as the fabric onto which the pieces will be sewn.

*RIGHT: A gingham draw-string bag makes the perfect base on which to sew a large patchwork piece embroidered with an old-fashioned jug and basin.
OPPOSITE: The same motif, this time reduced, is combined with other bathroom accessories to decorate a wash basin skirt.*

- set square
- crewel (embroidery) needle size 6
- dressmaker's carbon paper
- embroidery hoop

## STITCHES USED

stem stitch

French knot (*wash basin skirt only*)

back stitch (*wash basin skirt only*)

straight stitch (*draw-string bag only*)

running stitch

For full details on stitches see pages 132–7.

## TECHNIQUES

For full practical information on methods used in this project, see pages 129–31.

### To work the wash basin skirt

On a photocopier, enlarge the templates for the mirror and brush (see left) to 180% and the perfume bottle and jug to 130%. Using dressmaker's carbon paper, transfer the designs onto the cotton sheeting. The number of times you transfer each design will depend on the number of patchwork pieces you require. For a larger skirt or area of fabric, either transfer more motifs than the eight I used, at roughly the same distance apart, or enlarge the motifs, thus giving bigger patchwork pieces. When transferring the motifs, be sure to leave enough space around each one to allow for cutting out and hemming the patchwork pieces.

All the motifs are worked with three strands of thread. Referring to the photographs for the use of colour, work each motif as follows.

all the inner detail is complete, embroider the outline of the bottle in mid blue.

## HAIRBRUSH

The motif is worked entirely in stem stitch. Work the bristles of the brush first in pale blue – the direction of the stitches is unimportant – followed by the outline of the brush in mid blue. Next work a second row of stem stitch in lilac along the near edge for shading, before completing the inner detail.

## MIRROR

The motif is worked entirely in stem stitch. Start by stitching the whole outline in mid blue and the two inner oval shapes in mid blue and pale blue. Where indicated by the thicker lines of the template, embroider a second row of stitches inside the outline in lilac, as close to it as possible, for shading. Finish by making two more rows of stitches between the two oval shapes in lilac.

## WATER JUG AND BOWL

Start by stitching the diamond pattern, outlining the diamonds with stem stitch in pale blue (see 1 right). In the centre of each of these diamonds outline each smaller diamond with four back stitches in lilac. For the dotted rows, embroider French knots. Working in stem stitch only, embroider the double horizontal rows above and below the diamond pattern, before outlining the whole motif in mid blue. Note that the part of the outline marking the back of the jug rim is worked in lilac for contrast. The direction of the stitches is unimportant.

## PERFUME BOTTLE

The perfume bottle motif is worked entirely in stem stitch. Start by stitching the glass detail in pale blue and lilac, working all the vertical lines first. When

1

*LEFT: To outline the diamond pattern of the water jug, first work stem stitch in a continuous zig-zag line, as shown, from one side of the jug to the other. Turn and work back towards where you started. At the point where this second line crosses the first, simply stitch over the top of the first line.*

With a ruler and set square, mark out a square or rectangle round each motif, making sure the embroidery is centred within it. The size of each piece is largely dependent on the size of each motif as well as on the size of your skirt and the scale of

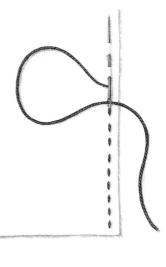

**2**

the checked fabric. For a more interesting design try to vary the sizes of these squares and rectangles. Add 1.5cm (⅝in) all round for hemming, then cut out. Turn the hem allowance under, cut off the corners diagonally to remove excess fabric, and press well.

### To make up the wash basin skirt

Turn under a double 12mm (½in) hem at the two side edges. Turn over the top edge by 4cm (1½in) and machine two lines of stitching (one 6mm/¼in and the other 2.5cm/1in from the top) to form a channel for the hanging wire. Turn under and stitch a 4cm (1½in) hem on the lower edge of the skirt.

Lay the skirt flat on the floor and randomly arrange the embroidered pieces on it. When you are satisfied with their arrangement, pin and tack them into position. Using three strands of lilac embroidery thread, secure the pieces all round with a row of running stitches (see 2 above).

### To work the draw-string bag

Enlarge the jug and bowl template on page 116 to 210% on a photocopier. Transfer the design onto the sheeting with dressmaker's carbon paper.

Unless stated otherwise, the motif is worked using six strands of thread. As for the jug and bowl motif described on page 117, start by stitching the diamond pattern in stem stitch, using three strands of thread in pale blue and lilac. This time, however, work the inner diamonds in stem stitch rather than back stitch, and replace the French knots with tiny crosses (see photograph right), formed from two straight stitches, one diagonally over the other. Work the banding lines in stem stitch in lilac then outline the jug and bowl in stem stitch with mid blue thread, using lilac for the back of the jug rim.

With a ruler and set square mark out a rectangle 20 x 22cm (8 x 8½in) around the design. Make sure the design is centred. Add a 1.5cm (⅝in) hem allowance all round, then cut out. Turn this under, cutting the corners diagonally, and press.

### To make up the draw-string bag

Cut out two pieces of checked fabric 35 x 63cm (14 x 25in), adding a 2cm (¾in) seam allowance all round. Position the embroidery on the front of one piece, 7.5cm (3in) from the lower edge (excluding the seam allowance). Pin and tack. Using three strands of mid blue thread, secure all round with a row of running stitches (see 2 opposite), making sure the stitches are evenly spaced and even in length.

With right sides facing, sew the back and front pieces together along the side and lower edges with 2cm (¾in) seams, leaving a 5cm (2in) opening on

one side for the cord, approximately 12cm (4¾in) from the top. Turn under a 2cm (¾in) hem on the top edge. Turn the bag to the right side and fold over the top to the inside so that the fold line falls mid-way along the opening. Stitch a 2.5cm (1in) channel along the top edge to hold the cord. The stitching line will pass just under the opening for the cord. Thread the cord through the channel and knot the ends together.

COLOUR GUIDE

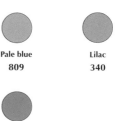

Pale blue
809

Lilac
340

Mid blue
3807

# AFTERNOON TEA

Part of the fun of embroidery is that it is so easy to alter a design; simply by varying the stitches you can create very different effects. A cup and saucer outlined in back stitch and chain stitch with lazy daisy flowers has a more delicate appearance than a cup and saucer boldly embroidered with long and short stitch. The floral cup and saucer design also has more fine detail, and so lends itself well to being enlarged.

*OPPOSITE: For the table-mat, the flowers on the teacup are replaced with solid bands of long and short stitch.*
*BELOW: The tea-cosy makes a beautiful frame for the cup and saucer motif.*

## MATERIALS

- DMC stranded cotton in the following colours:

  *For the tea-cosy*
    mid pink 335
    paler pink 962
    plum 3802
    yellow 3822
    green 3348

  *For the table-mat*
    mid pink 335
    green 3348

  One skein of each colour is plenty for both projects.

*For the tea-cosy*
- 40cm (16in) of cream cotton or linen fabric
- 50cm (20in) of thinner white or cream cotton fabric for lining
- 50cm (20in) square of wadding
- brown paper for making tea-cosy pattern
- tailor's chalk

*For the table-mat*
- 50cm (20in) square of medium to heavy cream cotton or linen

*For both projects*
- set square
- tracing paper
- crewel (embroidery) needle size 6
- dressmaker's carbon paper
- embroidery hoop

## STITCHES USED

*For the tea-cosy*
    lazy daisy stitch
    French knot
    straight stitch
    chain stitch
    back stitch

*For the table-mat*
    long and short stitch
    stem stitch
    chevron stitch
For full details on stitches, see pages 132–7.

## TECHNIQUES

For full information, see pages 129–31.

### To work the tea-cosy

First mark out on paper a squared-off version of your tea-cosy shape, using the size of your teapot as a guide. Cut out your rectangle and fold it in half

lengthwise. Starting from the bottom corner away from the fold, draw a freehand curved line up and over to the top of the fold. When you are happy with the shape, cut it out and unfold the paper to give the full tea-cosy shape. Using this template, mark out two tea-cosy shapes on the cotton or linen fabric. Add a 2.5cm (1in) seam allowance all round and cut out. Put one piece aside for the backing.

Enlarge the tea cup template below to the size of your choice on a photocopier. Using dressmaker's carbon paper, transfer the design on to the centre of the tea-cosy.

The entire design is worked with six strands of thread. Work the floral pattern first, referring to the photographs for the use of colour. Each flower head is made up of six lazy daisy stitches (or four where only part of the flower is visible) radiating evenly from its centre. Into the centre of each, work one French knot. The crosses between each flower are made up of four straight stitches. Except for the outer rim of the cup and saucer, which are worked in chain stitch, the remaining outline is in back stitch.

TEMPLATE

COLOUR GUIDE

| Mid pink | Paler pink | Plum | Yellow | Green |
|---|---|---|---|---|
| **335** | **962** | **3802** | **3822** | **3348** |

## To make up the tea-cosy

Place the embroidered and backing fabric pieces right sides together and, using a sewing machine or small back stitches, join along the curved edge. Hem both sides of the bottom edge and turn the cosy right side out. Press.

Use the paper template to mark out four tea-cosy shapes on the lining fabric. Add a 2.5cm (1in) hemming allowance along the bottom, and cut out. Mark out two pieces of wadding to match, but do not add any seam or hem allowances. Cut out. With right sides of one pair of linings together, pin, tack and machine stitch a 1.5cm (⅝in) seam along the curve. Repeat for the other pair. Turn one of the linings right side out and put the second inside it.

Assemble the under-cosy by pushing the two pieces of wadding in between the lining layers. Turn in the bottom edges of both linings and hand sew together. To keep the wadding in position, hand sew a few random stitches right through the lining and the wadding. For each stitch, oversew a few times in each place and finish off before starting the next stitch. The thread should not pass from one stitch to the other. When the wadding is attached, slip the padded under-cosy inside the embroidered cosy.

## To work the table-mat

Using a set square and ruler, mark out a rectangle 35 x 25cm (14 x 10in). Add a 4cm (1½in) hemming allowance all round and cut out. Press this hem under whilst working out the placement of the cups and chevron lines.

Trace or photocopy the template opposite and transfer it onto each of the table-mat corners (see

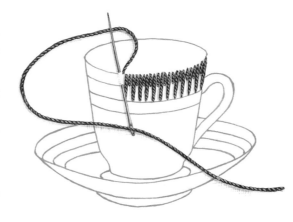

photograph on page 121) using dressmaker's carbon paper. Remember not to include the flower pattern when tracing and transferring the design; instead replace it with two extra lines (see illustration above).

The entire design is worked with four strands of thread. Work the solid areas of colour first in long and short stitch. Embroider round the top edge of the cup, using the first line below the rim as a guide for the length of the short stitches and the next line as a guide for the long stitches (see illustration above). When one row of long and short stitches has been completed, work a second row below this first row, embroidering short stitches below long, and long stitches below short. Repeat for the saucer.

Complete the cups and saucers by working all outlines in stem stitch. Embroider a line of chevron stitch between each cup, 3cm (1¼in) from the mat edge (see photograph on page 121). To help keep the chevron stitches even, first work a row of running stitches along the line to be embroidered. Remove this guideline when the embroidery is complete. Hem the table-mat with neat hand stitches.

# Techniques and Stitches

## FABRICS FOR EMBROIDERY

Apart from very loosely woven fabrics, almost any fabric can be used for embroidery. However, the choice of fabric will be dictated largely by the use of the finished item. For those that will be frequently washed, for example an embroidered tablecloth or hand towel, linen is an ideal choice. This strong fabric launders well, looking fresh time and time again, and with no distortion of the design. Always pre-wash fabric if the item will have to be laundered, so that any shrinkage occurs at this stage.

Other factors to consider when choosing fabric are the style of the design and the yarn. A design with fine outlines and delicate details to be embroidered in a stranded silk requires a smooth-surfaced and closely woven fabric. A simpler, bolder design using thicker thread works best on a heavier, even textured, and more loosely woven fabric. The looseness of weave will allow the thickness of the needle and thread to pass smoothly through the fabric without leaving any holes showing.

Nearly all of the projects in this book were made using linen and cotton. Both these fabrics are known as even-weave fabrics, which means they have an equal number of threads (warp and weft) in each direction. This evenness of weave minimizes distortion and pulling during stitching, which is particularly important where dense stitching occurs, making linen and cotton

ideal for embroidery. Both fabrics are widely available, and come in a range of different thicknesses, textures and colours.

## EMBROIDERY THREADS

Just as almost any fabric can be used for embroidery, so, too, can most threads, from silks, cottons and linens to wools – even string. Whichever thread you choose, it is essential that it is appropriate to the design. Stitches worked in different threads or thicknesses of thread will take on a very different appearance. A line of stem stitch worked in silk has a delicate appearance, while the same stitch worked in a thicker, twisted thread looks bolder and more dramatic. For this reason stranded cotton is the most commonly used embroidery

thread. It is made up of six fine strands that can be separated to create different thicknesses of thread and can be used on any type of fabric. Stranded cotton comes in an enormous selection of colours and is widely available. Because of its versatility and wonderful silky sheen (which have earned it its other name – embroidery silk), I chose to use it for the majority of the projects in this book.

The other cotton embroidery thread I have used is Coton Perlé (pearl cotton). This is a slightly twisted thread and is the most satiny of the embroidery threads. The strands cannot be separated but it is available in several thicknesses (or 'gauges') – 3, 5, 8 and 12, of which 3 is the thickest.

When buying thread for the projects in this book, remember that the amounts given are only approximate and will vary from one person to another, depending on how close together the stitches are worked, how much thread is used in starting and finishing, and the tension of the stitching. If you wish to duplicate my embroidery designs exactly, buy the same colour, brand and weight of embroidery thread as given in the 'Materials' list. If you wish to substitute threads of another brand, use the conversion chart on page 143 or, better still, experiment with different threads and colours. By trying out ideas on a spare piece of fabric you will learn how different threads, fabrics and stitches work together.

## NEEDLES

The importance of using the right needle for embroidery cannot be over-stressed. The most common needle for embroidery is a crewel needle. It has a sharp point which pierces the fabric easily and a long, slender eye. These needles are available in a range of sizes from 1 to 10; the lower the number, the larger the needle. It is important that the eye of the needle is sufficiently large to allow the thread to pass through smoothly without fraying. However, the threaded needle must not be too thick to pass through the fabric. If a needle leaves large holes in a fabric, use a finer one.

Within time all needles will start to loose their shiny plating. When this happens, and the needle feels sticky and appears tarnished, change it for a new one.

## FRAMES

Everyone should work embroidery in the way that they feel most comfortable – some people prefer to use a frame, which holds the fabric taut, while others find it easier to work the fabric in their hands. However, for working a sequence of satin stitches (see page 86), a frame is essential.

The most commonly used frame for embroidery is a hoop frame. They come in a range of sizes, but the basic design is the same, consisting of two wooden hoops that fit one inside the other. The fabric (at the area where you will be working) is laid over

the smaller hoop and the larger hoop is placed over the top. This pulls the fabric taut and even. A screw on the larger hoop adjusts the tension to keep the fabric stretched. For large pieces of embroidery where a design is too big to fit into the area of the hoop, the hoop can be moved around. It is important to remove the hoop in between periods of work, otherwise it can stretch the fabric permanently and also mark it.

As there are many different types of frame to choose from, I would suggest that you visit your local needlework shop where the staff will be able to advise which frame, if any, is the most suitable for you.

## ADDITIONAL EQUIPMENT

In addition to needles and frames, few other tools are required for successful embroidery. A pair of small, very sharp pointed embroidery scissors is essential, as is a larger pair for cutting fabric. For transferring patterns onto fabric you will need tracing paper and dressmaker's carbon or transfer paper. The latter is a non-smudge carbon paper that is available in several colours. Always choose a colour that contrasts well with the colour of your fabric, so that the working lines are clearly visible. For marking fine details directly onto the fabric use a water-soluble marking pen. And lastly, but perhaps most importantly, a good light source is essential if you want to avoid straining your eyes.

## TRANSFERRING THE PATTERN

After choosing the design you wish to embroider and gathering your materials, the next stage is to transfer the design onto the fabric. Each project in this book includes a template or line drawing of the design(s). In some cases these templates are actual size and all you need do is trace the pattern using tracing paper. Other templates have been reduced in scale to fit into the format of the book, and it is necessary to enlarge them to the right size. This is very easily done on a photocopier, and the relevant percentages are given where this is required.

The simplest way to transfer a design onto fabric is to use dressmaker's carbon paper, and this is the method I have used throughout this book. Note that before you start any stitching, it is important to transfer the whole design. This point cannot be over-emphasized, particularly when you are working repeat patterns that join up (see Garlands of Flowers on pages 18–21), because once stitching has started, it is very difficult to line up a pattern successfully.

Before transferring the design onto the fabric, press the fabric so that it is completely smooth. Place it right side up on a flat, hard surface and, if necessary, hold it in position with masking tape. Place the carbon paper, shiny side down, on the fabric, and use masking tape to secure it. Place the traced or photocopied design on top of the carbon paper and tape it into position. Pressing hard, trace carefully over the design with a fine ballpoint pen. If you press too lightly, the carbon paper lines will not only be too faint to work with, but will also be more likely to brush off before the embroidery is complete. Be careful not to lean on the carbon paper, as it does have a tendency to smudge. When the tracing is complete, carefully remove both the carbon and pattern papers. The fabric is now ready for you to embroider.

When working your embroidery, try to make sure that the stitches cover the carbon paper lines fully, so that no carbon shows when the embroidery is complete. If any lines do show, however, a quick wash will easily remove them.

Sometimes I like to work a design or detail of a pattern directly onto the fabric, thus by-passing the use of carbon paper. For this I use a water-soluble pen. Do not be tempted to use a pencil – the lead will dirty the embroidery thread.

## STARTING AND FINISHING WORK

An embroidery thread should be cut no longer than 50cm (20in). Longer lengths are more difficult to work with because they tend to twist and knot. When starting to work, leave a 2.5cm (1in) loose end at the back of the fabric and catch it down with the first few stitches. Knots should always be avoided in embroidery. When finishing off, the end of the thread should be run through the back of the last few stitches on the wrong side. Once the thread has been secured in this way, you can cut off any excess.

Where you start to stitch is, I think, largely a matter of personal preference. I like to work the outline of a motif first and then fill in the centre. If you make a mistake during stitching, take extra care when unpicking the stitches, otherwise you risk damaging the fabric. Carefully snip each wrong stitch with a pair of small, sharp pointed scissors and gently pull out the cut ends, using tweezers if necessary.

## WASHING EMBROIDERY

Embroidery is best washed in plenty of hot water and mild detergent. If the ends have been well worked in when starting and finishing, the fabric has been pre-shrunk and the colours are fast, there is nothing to fear. I even put my large pieces of embroidery into the washing machine, though I am careful not to over-spin. Do not tumble dry embroidery; instead, gently straighten it out and hang it up to dry. While the embroidery is still damp, press it on the wrong side. To avoid flattening stitches when pressing, place a thick towel or an old sheet folded several times over the ironing board and place the embroidery on top. If the embroidery is too dry, place a damp cloth over the work before starting to press.

# Stitches

The embroidery stitches described and illustrated here are some of the most elementary and frequently used, and they are all you will need to complete the projects in this book. Each one can be applied to any design, whether floral, geometric, or pictorial, and can be worked with all types of embroidery silks, cottons, stranded cottons, or embroidery wools.

## BACK STITCH

While running stitch (see page 136) produces a broken line of stitches, back stitch makes a more solid line. If the stitches are kept very small, back stitch can outline any shape, however awkward, which makes it ideal for embroidering fine details, such as tiny stems and leaf tendrils.

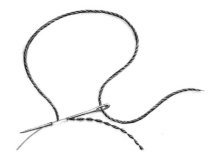

### To work

Working from right to left, bring the needle up through to the right side of the fabric and make a short backward stitch along the working line. With the needle now at the back of the work, take a long stitch forward and bring the needle up to the left of the backward stitch. The long stitch should be twice the length of the backward stitch. Take another short backward stitch on top, joining with the last stitch, and repeat in this way for the required distance. The stitches on top should be equal in length, with no gaps left between them.

## BLANKET STITCH

Blanket stitch is frequently used along the edges of household linens and blankets (hence the name) to add a decorative and colorful trim, as well as to secure raw edges. By varying the length and angle of the stitches, numerous different decorative effects can be achieved.

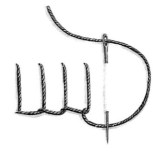

### To work

Blanket stitch is worked between parallel lines with the stitches all one length. Working from left to right, bring the thread through on the bottom line and hold it down with the left thumb. Insert the needle to the right on the top line and bring it out on the bottom line immediately below, with the point of the needle over the held thread, i.e., the loop. Pull the needle through until the thread lies flat on the material with the loop pulled tight. Continue working toward the right. When the stitches are worked closely together, this is called buttonhole stitch.

## CHAIN STITCH

Chain stitch is made by working a series of single looped stitches together in a line, with each stitch linking into the loop of the previous one. It is a very neat and simple stitch and is particularly effective as an outline stitch (see pages 30–35).

### To work

Bring the needle through at the point where the first stitch is to be and hold the thread down toward you with the left thumb. Insert the needle again just to the right of where the thread first emerged, then take a downward stitch of the required length. Pass the thread under the point of the needle and pull the needle through until the loop lies flat. Hold the thread down and again insert the needle just to the right of the emerging thread and inside the loop already made. Work a stitch of the same length as the previous one, and continue the chain in this way.

## CHEVRON STITCH

Chevron stitch is worked between two parallel lines and from left to right. It is most frequently used as a border stitch, but also works well as a filling stitch when it is embroidered in rows.

### To work

**1.** Beginning at the left-hand end of the lower line, make a back stitch (see page 132), with the needle emerging for the second stitch halfway along this stitch.

**2.** Working to the right, take the needle to the top line and, with it pointing to the left, make a small stitch.

**3.** Make a back stitch to the right along the top line, emerging again halfway back along the stitch.

**4.** Take the needle back down to the bottom line and form the bottom stitch in the same way as shown for the top stitch in steps 2 and 3. Continue in this way, alternating between the bottom and top lines to create a zig-zag effect.

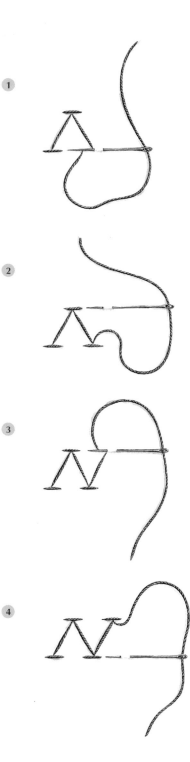

## COUCHING STITCH

When loose threads are stitched down with another thread, this is known as couching. There are many ways in which the threads can be held in place, but for the purpose of this book I have worked couching stitch only in its simplest form (see pages 76–9).

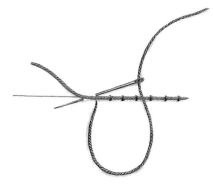

### To work

Bring the thread that is to be stitched down through to the right side of the fabric and lay it along the line to be worked. Hold securely in place with the left hand. With another needle and finer thread, work tiny and evenly spaced vertical stitches along the length of the first thread to keep it in place.

## FERN STITCH

Fern stitch is made up of three single stitches radiating from a central line. All three stitches should be equal, but their size depends on the design. It is useful for delicate, fern-like sprays (see pages 18–21) and for the veins of leaves.

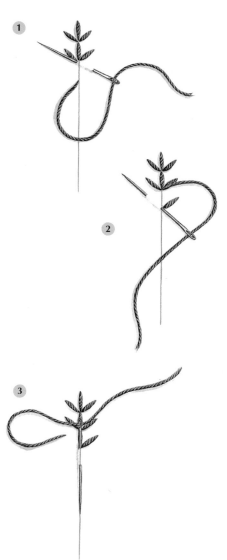

### To work

**1.** Mark the length of one stitch down the central working line and bring the needle through at the bottom point of the stitch. Work one single stitch to the right, at a 45-degree angle to the central line, and then point the needle back towards the left, and bring it out at the top of the central working line.

**2.** Make a stitch down the central line, inserting the needle at the bottom of the first stitch. Make one single stitch to the left, similar in length and angle to the one on the right.

**3.** Pull the needle through, and take it back to the central line, inserting it where the first and second stitches meet. Take a stitch of the same length as the others down the central line. Continue as before for the required length.

### FLY STITCH

This very simple and versatile stitch can be worked in rows, groups or as a single detached stitch.

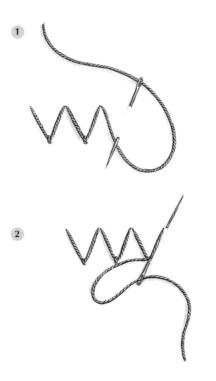

### FRENCH KNOT STITCH

A French knot looks like a small bead lying on a piece of fabric. This detached stitch can be worked to form a line or a group and is often used in embroidery to give focus to the centres of flowers (see pages 36–41) and to form the eyes of tiny animals and birds.

### LAZY DAISY STITCH

Lazy daisy is also known as detached chain stitch because each stitch stands alone. Each single chain stitch is secured at the top by a small stitch.

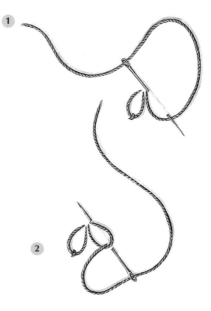

### To work

**1.** Bring the needle through at the point where the top of the stitch is to be and hold the thread down towards you. Insert the needle to the right and take a diagonal stitch downwards to the centre. Pull the needle through, keeping the thread under the point of the needle, until a V-shape is formed.
**2.** Insert the needle just below the thread, making a tiny vertical holding stitch. Bring the point out at the top of the next stitch.

### To work

**1.** Bring the needle through at the point where you want the knot to be. With the left hand, hold the thread taut. Wind the thread round the needle once or twice (depending on the size of knot you want).
**2.** Turn the needle round and insert it into the fabric close to where the thread first emerged, still keeping the thread taut. Pull the needle through, releasing the thread at the very last minute.

### To work

**1.** Bring the needle through at the point where the top of the first stitch is to be and hold the thread down towards you with the left thumb. Insert the needle again just to the right of where the thread first emerged, then take a downwards stitch of the required length.
**2.** Pass the thread under the needle point and pull the needle through until the thread lies flat. Put the needle in again just beneath the loop to make a small vertical holding stitch. Repeat for each stitch.

## LONG AND SHORT STITCH

Long and short stitch is used to cover large areas with thread. Only the first row consists of long and short straight stitches, the following rows being worked in even-length stitches (except where the outline restricts their size). The blended effect makes the stitch ideal for shading.

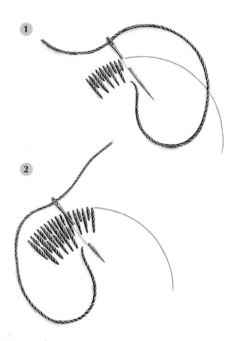

### To work

**1.** First work a row of straight stitches, alternating long and short. Keep the outer edge of the shape even.

**2.** Work a row of even-length stitches into the short stitches of the first row, passing the needle through the tip of the stitch above. Continue with rows of even-length stitches until the required area is filled.

## RUNNING STITCH

This stitch is identical to the running stitch used in sewing. It consists of short stitches running in and out of the fabric in a single line. It is the perfect stitch for outline work, in particular where a broken line, rather than a heavier, solid one, is required.

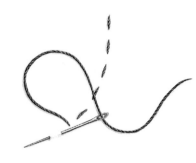

### To work

Working from right to left, pass the needle in and out of the fabric to create a broken line of stitches along the line to be worked. It is important to keep the stitches and the spaces between the stitches even. The resulting effect depends not only on the size of the stitches but also on the thickness of thread used (the thicker the embroidery thread, the larger the stitch).

## SATIN STITCH

Satin stitch is the most commonly used stitch for filling an area with solid colour. The stitches are worked evenly from one side of the shape to the other and are so close together that no fabric shows through. Satin stitch is ideal for smaller shapes such as petals and leaves, but less suitable for large areas, where the effect can be loose and untidy. One solution for large areas is to work several rows of satin stitch, but I would usually recommend using some other filling stitch such as long and short stitch.

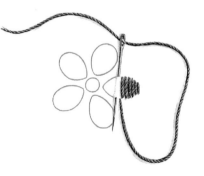

### To work

Bring the needle through from the wrong side at the lower edge of the space to be filled, insert it at the top edge and bring the needle out again at the bottom, close to the thread. The first stitch, which can be either upright or sloping, sets the angle for all following stitches. All stitches must be parallel, without overlapping, and should be smooth and neat.

### PADDED SATIN STITCH

For a raised effect, the area to be covered in satin stitch is first padded. When the stitches are made, the light catches on the curves of the padding to create an extra richness and depth of colour.

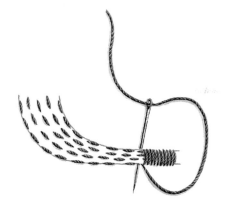

### STEM STITCH

Stem stitch is one of the most widely used stitches in embroidery, and is sometimes known as crewel or outline stitch. The stitches slightly overlap one another to produce an unbroken and very smooth running line. This makes it particularly good for creating curves.

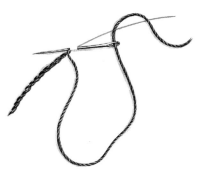

### STRAIGHT STITCH

Straight stitch, also known as stroke or single stitch, is simply one single, flat stitch and is the basis of many other stitches. The stitches can be grouped in many different ways to create simple shapes (see pages 70–75) or worked detached from any neighbouring stitch to add detail to a design.

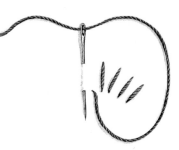

### To work

First work a row of small running stitches inside the outline of the shape to be filled, then fill the area inside with further rows of running stitches. Now work satin stitch over this padding.

### To work

Bring the needle through to the right side of the fabric, just to the left of the working line. Take the needle a little way along the working line and, with it pointing back towards the left, insert it just to the right of the line, making a stitch at a slight angle across the line. Pull the needle through and repeat, keeping the length and angle of the stitches even. The stitch can be worked with the thread to either the right or the left of the needle, but it must be consistent

Altering the angle of the stitches can vary the thickness of the line. For fine lines, pass the needle directly along the working line. For a thicker effect, pass it on either side.

### To work

Bring the needle through to the right side of the fabric and make one stitch of any length and in any direction. If several stroke stitches are to be worked near one another, bring the needle out each time in the right place to make the next stitch.

# Index

THE DESIGNS IN THIS BOOK were embroidered with DMC stranded embroidery cotton. If you prefer to work in Anchor embroidery cotton, refer to the conversion chart below. It lists all the DMC shades used, followed by the nearest equivalent Anchor shade available. These alternatives, however, are only approximate equivalents and will therefore give a slightly different effect from that shown in the pictures. Both DMC and Anchor threads are widely available in department stores and needlework shops. If you have problems finding a stockist near you, contact the relevant distributor listed below.

**DMC** - Anchor

| | | | | | | | |
|---|---|---|---|---|---|---|---|
| **210** - 108 | **349** - 13 | **503** - 875 | **720** - 326 | **783** - 306 | **962** - 75 | **3348** - 254 | **3805** - 63 |
| **211** - 342 | **350** - 11 | **553** - 98 | **721** - 324 | **791** - 178 | **973** - 290 | **3607** - 87 | **3806** - 62 |
| **304** - 19 | **367** - 262 | **554** - 96 | **722** - 323 | **798** - 131 | **987** - 262 | **3608** - 86 | **3807** - 122 |
| **309** - 39 | **368** - 261 | **606** - 334 | **726** - 295 | **799** - 130 | **988** - 261 | **3687** - 76 | **3819** - 278 |
| **321** - 47 | **436** - 363 | **666** - 46 | **727** - 293 | **809** - 130 | **989** - 261 | **3705** - 35 | **3820** - 306 |
| **335** - 38 | **470** - 267 | **676** - 886 | **729** - 890 | **815** - 1005 | **3041** - 871 | **3746** - 110 | **3821** - 305 |
| **336** - 150 | **471** - 265 | **704** - 256 | **738** - 942 | **913** - 203 | **3051** - 861 | **3779** - 868 | **3822** - 295 |
| **340** - 1030 | **472** - 254 | **712** - 926 | **743** - 305 | **946** - 330 | **3347** - 266 | **3802** - 897 | **3823** - 292 |

DMC Coton Perlé No 5 shade **712** - Anchor Pearl Cotton shade 2

## Distributors

**DMC**

UK
DMC Creative World
Pullman Road
Wigston, Leicester
LE18 2DY
Tel: 01162 811040

AUSTRALIA
DMC Needlecraft Pty Ltd
51-66 Carrington Road
Marrickville, NSW 2204
Tel: 02 559 3088

JAPAN
DMC K.K.
3-7-4-203 Kuramae
Taito-Ku
Tokyo 11
Tel: 3 582 84112

NEW ZEALAND
Warnaar Trading Co Ltd
376 Ferry Road
PO Box 19567
Christchurch
Tel: 03 89288

SOUTH AFRICA
S.A.T.C.
43 Somerset Road
PO Box 3868
Capetown 8000
Tel: 2 141 980 40

**ANCHOR**

UK
Coats Crafts UK
McMullen Road
Darlington, County
Durham DL1 1YQ
Tel: 01325 365457

AUSTRALIA
Coats Patons Crafts
89-91 Peters Avenue
Mulgrave, Victoria 3170
Tel: 61 39 561 2288

JAPAN
Dynacast (Japan) Ltd
4-19-30 Nobidome
Niiza City
Saitama Prefecture 352
Tel: 81484 811277

NEW ZEALAND
Coats Enzed Crafts
40 Sir William Avenue
East Tamaki
Tel: 64 9 274 01 16

SOUTH AFRICA
Coats Natal Thread
Kelly Road
Hammarsdale, Natal 3700
Tel: 27 325 62171

# Acknowledgments

**Author's** THIS BOOK WOULD NOT HAVE BEEN POSSIBLE WITHOUT THE HELP AND COMMITMENT OF SUCH A WONDERFUL TEAM OF PEOPLE.

A very big thank you to Carolyn Jenkins for her beautifully precise illustrations; to Alison Bolus for her meticulous checking and rechecking of text; and to Jane Moran, Rosalind Fairman and Marie Willey, who were so generous in allowing us to invade their homes and gardens for photography. I would also like to extend a special thanks to Tessa Clayton for her help, and to Cara Ackerman at DMC.

I am, as always, indebted to Fiona Lindsay, my agent, for her constant guidance, and to Suzannah Gough for inviting me to join Conran Octopus.

In particular, I wish to thank Alison Barclay for designing such an exquisite book, and Helen Ridge for not only pulling the whole book together but for her unending support and patience. A very special thank you to Sandra Lane, who took all the glorious photographs and with whom I had such fun.

Thank you, Charles, as always, for your enormous support and constant encouragement.

**Publisher's** The publisher would like to thank Andrew Whiteley – The Inkshed for the calligraphy on the jacket and chapter openers, and King & King for the alphabets on pages 88 and 89. Thanks, also, to The Blue Door, 77 Church Road, London SW13 (Tel: 0181 748 9785) for the checked fabric used in the Border of Crosses project; the wool blanket in the Sprinkled Snowflakes project; and the blue linen in the Delicate Posies project.